People
in the
Pews

Sarah Williams

People
in the
Pews

Modern Stories of God's Love and Grace

SARAH WILLIAMS

XULON PRESS

Xulon Press
2301 Lucien Way #415
Maitland, FL 32751
407.339.4217
www.xulonpress.com

Unless otherwise indicated, Scripture quotations taken from The Holy Bible:
International Standard Version. Release 2.0, Build 2015.02.09. Copyright ©
1995-2014 by ISV Foundation. ALL RIGHTS RESERVED INTERNATIONALLY.
Used by permission of Davidson Press, LLC.

Printed in the United States of America

Paperback ISBN-13: 978-1-6628-0589-9
Ebook ISBN-13: 978-1-6628-0590-5

Dedication

This book is dedicated to the incredible men and women who were willing to bare their souls so that others may find God. Thank you for sharing your past, present, and hopes for the future with me. Without you, this book would not have been possible. Working with you and hearing your stories have forever changed my life.

To my husband, JT. Thank you for your love, patience, and guidance as I embarked on this journey. I am so blessed to have you by my side. To my daughters, Aubrey, Isabelle, and Faith. Being your mother is an immense blessing that I am thankful for daily. Your beautiful lives are what made me want to be a better person and live a better life.

Note from the Author

O ver the months of writing this book and growing in my faith, as well as my relationship with God, I felt conflicted about which version of the Bible to use for scriptural references. With so many translations I wanted to make sure I was using the one that best represented the original text. I prayed about it for many weeks as I came closer to the completion of the book. Just before working on the Scripture reference guide, I clearly heard a voice say, "I want them to know Me by *My* name."

Part of my growth in my faith has been reading a version of the Bible called, simply, The Scriptures. It's the Bible translated by the Institute for Scripture Research, which refers to God and Jesus by the original Hebrew translation of their names: Yahweh, Yahweh Elohim, and Yeshua. Once I heard that, I knew that all scriptural references would be from The Scriptures.

You will find outside of the Bible passages referenced, I still use the English translations for the names God, Jesus, Lord, and Christ.

I hope that reading Bible passages that translate God and Jesus as they were said during the times when the Bible was originally written brings you closer to Yahweh Elohim (the Lord our God) and Yeshua Hamashiach (Jesus the Messiah), as it has for me.

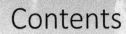

Contents

A Calling

For seven years, God placed a calling on my heart. Throughout those years, I would get random bursts of intense excitement. I didn't understand how I could be so excited for something I didn't know about, but I cherished those moments. They gave me a sense of expectancy for what was to come in my life. I didn't have the slightest idea what that calling may be, until late 2019. It wasn't until I gave up my "self" and relied solely on God that I began to see something manifest itself. Piece by piece, the puzzle started becoming clearer, and while I know there are still pieces that have yet to fall into place, I am starting to see His plan for me.

There is so much that precedes January 2020, but it was that month I began to pray to God to use me to serve Him and further His kingdom. You will learn throughout this book that me saying those words is a far cry from how I have lived 95 percent of my life. This prayer also didn't make sense in the physical dimension, because I didn't have a job that centered around God. It centered around educational travel. However, deep within my heart, I knew I wanted to spend my life serving Him. I prayed this prayer over and over for several months. God heard me and made it abundantly clear what I should do.

About a month prior to God telling me to write this book, I shared this on my social media account:

Today was my second time taking pictures for the church. I loved it even more than the first time. I am a people watcher, and part of the beauty of taking pictures is capturing incredible moments of people worshipping God. Now, don't get me wrong; I love getting my worship on, but when, on occasion, I take pictures, it's a whole different kind of worship for me. I get to marvel in the work God has done to people on an individual level. I get to see tears of joy and thankfulness for what He has done in people's lives. I get to see husbands, wives, parents, friends supporting each other in worship and giving their lives to God together.

I often wonder how people have come to know Him. Has it been a journey they embarked on as a child? Did they not begin to accept God until their twenties, thirties, forties, fifties, etc? Are they just starting their walk, or have they been growing in their faith for years? I guess it's the journalist in me that wants to ask all the questions—to learn about what led them to this moment and how far they've come. Because everyone has a story. None of us are perfect. My husband and I have made major mistakes. Personally, I strayed very far from God for many years. What are their stories—the people who sit in the seats beside me?

Since I have gotten more involved in the church, I have learned some of my fellow churchgoers' stories. All of us have walked a very different path, and each one of us, even filled with our mistakes, are beautiful because of the healing power of Jesus Christ. The journalist in me again would love to share some of their stories, because I often hear people say they are too far gone or they did this, that, and the other thing, so there's no way they will be forgiven. Or they are like me and just question everything. But there are people I sit with every Sunday and Wednesday that have stories of redemption. There are answers. There are stories of love. They are people who truly want the best and to help bring more people to Jesus. Not because they were told they should do it but because they allowed God to step into their lives and change them. Myself included. I want you to know you are not alone. There is not a perfect person in the pews. But there are people who are forgiven, have forgiven themselves, and continue to grow and learn."

Just a few weeks after writing this post, the country began shutting down over Covid-19. The travel industry, my job, took a huge hit. All the places I was supposed to go—Philadelphia, New Orleans, and Williamsburg—were shut down. My travel season, which was to start in March, ended, and there was a major slowdown in my day-to-day, job-related duties. This abrupt halt allowed me to continue to go to church on days I would normally have been traveling for work.

Much like many other Wednesday's prior, I was sitting in church listening to the pastor preach, but this Wednesday was a little different. Fewer people were in attendance. Everyone was sitting a little farther apart than usual, even though we all still greeted each other and chatted before service. This was also the first Wednesday night that I would be in the Prayer Center. I remember sitting there looking at the people sitting in the pews. Some I had gotten to know during the five months we had attended the church. Others I had only smiled at. I wondered how many more times I would be sitting with them before the inevitable would happen, and I wondered how long after that it would take before we were in person again. Little did I know, that was the last night we would physically be in the church for two months.

I decided to turn my full attention back to the pastor. Afterall, I was there to learn, not to ponder the future, and I had notes to take. I wrote what my pastor was saying in my notebook. "This is not the time to tuck our tails and run." Shortly after that I heard, "You need to write a book." If I could have laughed out loud, I would have, because as I heard that, the pastor was saying, "There is a higher power we need to follow."

So I say in my own mind, "Okay, God. That's great, but what do you want me to write about? Can't have a book without a subject."

He said, "You need to share their stories: the people in the pews."

At that point it took everything in me not to jump out of my seat and drive home to tell my husband. I still wrote lots of notes on what the pastor was talking about after the conversation with God, but to say I was a wee bit distracted would be an understatement. I was still volunteering in the Prayer Center after church too. That would be an additional thirty minutes after service before I could go home. I knew I would need to focus on the people calling in for prayer. God was truly testing my ability to focus on the task at hand. Needless to say, once I got home, I was chattering a million miles an hour to my husband about what had happened. After I calmed myself, I grabbed the notebook I used for church and began to write down basic questions that I wanted each person I spoke with to answer. I was thrilled but at the same time terrified.

> *"For Elohim has not given us a spirit of cowardice,*
> *but of power and of love and of self-control"*
> *(2 Tim. 1:7).*

Sometimes, even when God speaks to you, you question the very words you hear. When God spoke to me telling me I was supposed to write a book that shared the story of the people in the pews, I was thrilled for the opportunity to share people's journeys and how they came to accept Jesus Christ as their Lord and Savior. I was thrilled to be able to use something I love doing, writing, to further the Kingdom. But then I began to question myself. How was I going to reach out to people and ask them to share their stories during a time when we're supposed to be socially distancing ourselves? Were people going to believe me, or were they going to think I'd lost my mind? Were people even going to be willing to share some of the hardest moments in their lives with, perhaps, a stranger? Was I worthy of the task at hand?

It took two solid days of questioning myself before I told myself to stop it. It had taken seven years and one heck of a personal journey for God to finally reveal my purpose, and I wasn't about to back out now. I will never forget praying to God, telling Him I was going to listen to Him and asking Him who he wanted me to reach out to. As people were placed on my heart, I began to message them, giving them a brief background as to why I was reaching out. To my excitement, I was met with many positive responses.

Rachel was the first who said, "I would love to talk with you!" Not only has God worked miracles in her life, but He used her to instill in me that I was doing the right thing. You see, the night God spoke to me and told me I was to write this book was the same night God spoke to her telling her that now was not the time to be silent about her story. Just a couple days later (the days I spent questioning myself) I messaged her, asking her to share her story.

God knew I would question myself. He knew I would be nervous. He knew I would need reassurance, because even with positive responses I was *still* questioning myself. He used Rachel to squash all those fears and insecurities. It was through her words and the blatant proof of God's will that I understood sharing these stories were important not just for you, the person reading these words, but for the men and women who shared their stories.

"Write in a book for yourself all the words that I have spoken to you" (Jer. 30:2).

There is something so incredibly powerful and raw in a testimony. It is the expression of one's darkest moments to share the light. It is using the utterance of fears, heart break, and tortured moments to share how God worked in someone's life. I heard the influx in people's voices. I saw facial expressions change when sharing some incredibly painful memories. I heard people say, "This is hard for me to do, but if it can help someone else out, I want to do it." But you know what I also heard? Hope, redemption, forgiveness, love, compassion, faith, mercy, thankfulness, relief.

God uses those who are "too far gone," the "we're not good enough," the "doubtful." Do you want to know why? Because you (if I could, I would point at you), the person reading this book, can reach others that I can't reach. Your story has power. Your story has purpose. Your story has the ability to reach into someone's heart and open up things they thought could never be reached. Your life has meaning beyond the everyday, mundane tasks we all drudge through. Your life has meaning beyond your current situation. God has a purpose for your life, and it is greater than you could ever imagine.

Chapter One
You Have a Purpose

What is the purpose of life? When I searched for that on the internet, between web pages, images, videos, books, news, and the more tab, there were 1.8 billion results. Let me repeat that—1.8 billion, with a *b*, results. I have a degree in journalism, so I'm all for a good research session, but that is a little overwhelming. Heck, that's really overwhelming. Who in the world wants to wade through twenty-four pages of web articles to try to find the purpose of life? Let me save you some time on where you should look on your purpose-filled quest. Go to the Bible and read God's word. Go to Him and prayerfully seek His guidance. You will be amazed at what He shows you.

Recently, I was reading the book of Esther. I had read it four other times over the last couple of years, but that week I was feeling drawn to read that specific book yet again. So I read the book for the fifth time. Upon this fifth time reading it, Esther 4:14 jumped out at me like a neon sign: "For if you keep entirely silent at this time, relief and deliverance shall arise for the Jews from another place, while you and your father's house perish. And who knows whether you have come to the reign for such a time as this?"

You might wonder why this jumped out at me, as I am not a Jew, nor am I royalty. When I read this, I was at a bit of a crossroads.

I wasn't wondering what the purpose of my life was, but I was in need of clarification when it came to life choices. This is how I understood the verse: "For if you keep entirely silent at this time, relief and deliverance shall arise for the Jews from another place, while you and your father's house perish." Now is not a time for me to be silent. I must raise the banner of God and share His Word. This is my chance to help.

"And who knows whether you have come to the reign for such a time as this?" My life experiences have helped me to get to this point. God created me to live now and for the purpose He is laying out in front of me.

When you dig into the word of God, He begins to reveal the answers to your questions. Even the answer to what is the purpose of your life. It may take time, even years, as you grow in your faith. You may even have to re-read a verse multiple times before its meaning truly hits you, but He will always guide you. Be patient and purposeful in your actions. Be open to new paths that He guides you down. Understand that your plans, however well laid, if not aligned with God's purpose for you, will falter, and your course will be changed. Do not think that you do not have a purpose. You do. Open up your heart to God and ask Him to show you the reason for your creation.

> *"Many plans are the plans in a man's heart, but it is the counsel of Yahweh that stands" (Prov. 19:21).*

Randall
> *"And do not be conformed to this world, but be transformed by the renewing of your mind, so that you prove what is that good and well-pleasing and perfect desire of Elohim" (Rom. 12:2).*

When I began writing this book, I prayed to God about the people I would ask to share their testimonies. I knew that there were people that were supposed to be in this book that I did not know. I asked God to bring those people to me or to guide me to them. Imagine my excitement when God connected me with two individuals that I had never met, with vastly different but incredibly beautiful testimonies of how God worked in their lives.

Randall was the second stranger brought to me by God. When I completed my interview with him, I could not believe how perfectly God had aligned each person and the expanse of which God's love moves in people's lives.

Growing up, Randall never gave much thought to God. It wasn't that he didn't believe. He just didn't care. While he did party and drink in his teens and early twenties, he never got into drugs or had anything he would consider dramatic happen to him. Up until he was twenty-three years old, he felt like he was living a pretty regular life.

At twenty-three, he started questioning everything. Was he going down the wrong path? What was the purpose of his life? Was there more to Christianity than he had originally thought?

During the time Randall was beginning to question many aspects of his life, he began working at a power plant. The hours were long, so it gave him time to get to know his coworkers, one of which was a younger guy who was a Christian. Randall asked his coworker why he was Christian and how he knew that God was the right God. His coworker...didn't have an answer to either of those questions.

When talking about this moment in his life, Randall told me he wasn't trying to question his coworkers faith or be disrespectful. He was truly curious. He felt let down, though, when his questions weren't answered. I believe this part of Randall's life is representative of so many people. We all have questions when we apply for a new job, buy a new car, or are looking at new homes. What makes being new in faith any different?

If you are already well into your faith walk, I want you to think about the questions Randall asked. Do you personally know why you are Christian or why God is the right God? If you had this question asked of you, could you answer it, and could you answer it in a way that brings clarity?

If you are new in your faith walk, don't be afraid to ask hard questions, but also be open to hearing answers you weren't expecting. God works in profound ways, and not every person will have the same testimony. Not every person will cite the same scripture even in response to the same exact question. Also, start thinking about how you would respond if these questions were asked of you, because someday they may be.

> *"Ask and it shall be given to you, seek and you shall find, knock and it shall be opened to you"* *(Matt. 7:7).*

Although Randall's questions were not initially answered, God heard his questions and was getting ready to answer them in a bold way.

There was an older man, Mr. James, who worked at the same power plant as Randall, who always brought his Bible to work and read it on his lunch break. Randall happened to be taking his lunch break at the same time and noticed that like all other lunch breaks Mr. James was reading his Bible. During this lunch break, there were several guys, varying in age, who were mocking Mr. James. They kept telling him that he was reading a book of fairytales. They began to pick out individual stories from the Bible and explain how false they were. Randall was disappointed with how disrespectful they were being, and he was amazed at Mr. James' response.

There was a sense of reverence in Randall's voice as he explained the five minutes that changed his life. Mr. James did not get mad. He did not raise his voice or start telling the young guys where they could go. With a completely calm attitude, he backed the Bible, and as Randall said, "completely destroyed their world view." He politely dismantled every argument or negative comment the young men had to say about the Bible. At this moment, Randall realized most of what he had learned or heard had been wrong. Randall was amazed that for every question or argument the young men had, Mr. James had an answer. When the men left, Randall began talking to Mr. James about the incident. Mr. James suggested Randall buy the Kent Hovind DVD set to get him started on his walk with God.

Days, weeks, and months passed. Randall remembered what happened in the break room, but he had set aside Mr. James's advice. Randall continued to drink and party. Almost two months after his interaction with Mr. James, Randall was involved in some things he shouldn't have been. For the first time in his life, though, he felt conflicted about his actions. This was a new and uncomfortable feeling for Randall.

The week he felt conflicted, he decided to go to his dad's house for a visit. They did the usual how's-life chat, watched some TV, and then Randall decided to go about his day. As he was walking to the back door, he heard his dad flipping through the channels on the TV. Right as Randall put his left hand on the doorknob to leave, he heard a voice coming from the TV: "Hi. I am Kent Hovind, and I believe the Bible to be true." Randall recognized the name from his conversation with Mr. James. He rushed back into the living room and asked his dad to turn back to the channel with Kent Hovind. He called Mr. James to confirm that he was remembering correctly. That day, Randall ordered the DVD set that Mr. James had told him about two months prior.

In one week, Randall had listened to every DVD in the seven-DVD set. He described it as a mind-blowing experience. He felt a sense of confusion, because many of the things he had thought he had known were wrong. He was hearing a side of Christianity that he had never heard before. It was almost overwhelming, but it allowed Randall to think deeper than he ever had before. He knew without a shadow of a doubt that there was a God and that he needed to start studying the Bible. He had a Bible his grandma had bought him as a child but knew he needed something more age appropriate. It was a very exciting moment for him when he bought his first Bible. He had a fire for God, and he wanted to learn all he could. Randall knew that he finally had what he needed in order to learn more about God.

As soon as that fire was lit, Randall began experiencing a battle he had never acknowledged until that time: Satan trying to hold him back. It was not easy for Randall to be a new believer in the environment he had surrounded himself with for years. He felt like he would be doing good in his walk with God, but then Satan would use the people around him to lead him to temptation. For every positive step forward in the next step he would find himself falling back into his old ways. Randall recognized his problems and called out to God in prayer. He asked God to remove him from temptation. He was tired of failing and knew he needed to make a change.

> *"Call unto Me, and I shall answer you, and show you great and inaccessible matters, which you have not known" (Jer. 33:3).*

God heard Randall and spoke to him: "Get your Bible." This was the first and (so far) only time Randall had heard God speak to him. He didn't take time to think about what God said or be in awe. He immediately grabbed his Bible and began to read. He didn't know where he was supposed to read. He started reading about society during the end times and realized that his circle of friends had started to grow distant when he became a Christian. He flipped through the Bible some more and came upon 2 Timothy 3:14: "But you, stay in what you have learned and trusted, having known from whom you have learned." It was at that moment he knew. Randall closed his Bible and never questioned God again. His walk with God was solidified and would do nothing but grow.

God heard Randall and gave him unwavering belief, but that is not all God did. He answered Randall's prayer to be removed from temptation. Shortly after he knew he was to unwaveringly walk with God, Randall was called to work at a power plant in Live Oak, FL. Live Oak is an incredibly rural area with very little to do, outside of enjoying the great outdoors. It has a very small population and was far enough away from where Randall had lived that he chose not to go home for visits. For one year, he lived in a camper in the woods with no TV and no cell service. Outside of work and going to the gym, he spent his time reading his Bible. Randall calls this period in his life his "season to grow roots" in his faith.

At first, living in the wilderness was weird and inconvenient for Randall. However, after some time it became peaceful. It changed his perspective. He enjoyed the quiet time and began to appreciate his time with God. He began reading the Gospels (Matthew, Mark, Luke, and John). It was through that reading that he really began to appreciate who God is and deepened his faith.

Nearly three hundred times, the word *wilderness* is translated in the Bible. Many of those three hundred times, God used the wilderness to draw people closer to him. It is a time where the individual (Moses, Elijah, Jesus, etc.) is separated from society. God used this time to allow their fear to be overcome by faith and to give them a renewed strength in their relationship with Him. While being in a literal wilderness today may not be as common as it was in the days of Moses, Elijah, and Jesus, God still creates those moments where people are drawn and held within the wilderness until they reach the point in their relationship with Him that they are supposed to be. Randall is proof that even in this modern world the wilderness still holds significance. Randall found peace, gained perspective, and his faith was deepened while being in the wilderness for one year.

Upon his return to his hometown, Randall found that all the friends he had prior to leaving had moved away. The ones who brought temptation into his life were no longer a part of his life. God was still answering his prayer. The second half of his prayer to remove temptation was to connect him with strong men of God who would help him grow. It took some time, but he found a church where several of the men were former coworkers including the preacher. The bad had been removed and the good was helping him grow.

Randall began to see his personality changing as well. His bad temper and self-centered tendencies began to subside. He felt a peace that he had never felt before in his life. He occasionally still struggled with a short temper but promptly apologized for his actions. Prior to accepting God into his life, he did not apologize. He also does not overreact like he used to. He believes that God has given him wisdom so that he can better share the Word of God.

He has also seen God provide for him time and time again. When the months came that he didn't know how he was going to make rent, something would always happen so that he was taken care of. "God would provide a way out of nowhere." When those that were close to him were battling drug addiction, Randall was able to use what he had learned in his walk with God to minister to them. Many of which have begun to turn their lives around and begin to accept God into their lives as well. While Randall had seen God work in his life and the lives of others, there was one life Randall frequently prayed would be changed.

Randall's brother was much like Randall used to be. He just didn't care about God. Once Randall came home from his job in Live Oak, he would try to minister to his brother, but his brother would usually say, "When I am older, I'll start thinking about it." So Randall prayed, "Please, save my brother." He would pray that over and over again for a year and a half. Then one day, Randall received a call from his brother asking him to come take a walk with him. He could tell by the way his brother was talking it was urgent.

His brother, who worked in security, was at his job the night before. That night he went to the top of one of the towers of the site he was on. While he was up there, he felt an overwhelming presence. He was taken aback by how strong the presence felt. He began to feel a love like he had never felt before. Right there, in the middle of the night while he was working security, Randall's brother broke down and gave his life to God. He told Randall that he had been watching Randall for the last year and a half and had seen how God had changed him. Seeing how Randall had changed had begun to open his heart up to God. After his experience in the tower Randall's brother's life has never been the same. He lives his life, like Randall, for God. Randall's prayer was answered.

> *"Let your light so shine before men, so that they see*
> *your good works and praise your Father who is in*
> *the heavens" (Matt. 5:16).*

It has been six years since Randall began his walk with God. To say his life has changed would be an understatement. He has taken time to travel around Florida and minister to the homeless creating care packages for them including basic hygiene items as well as a Bible and some food items. He speaks to others about God as much as he can whether it is at work or in the community. He has had those who have disputed him, citing his age, twenty-nine, as their reluctance to listen to him. He believes, though, it is not really his age they are disputing. It is what he is sharing with them that makes them not want to listen. He doesn't let that stop him, though, and still tries to continue the conversation. He knows he is supposed to go out and preach the gospel. God has placed it on his heart to be an evangelist. He enjoys traveling so what could be better than traveling and sharing the word of God.

> *"For we are His workmanship, created in Messiah*
> *Yeshua unto good works, which Elohim pre-*
> *pared beforehand that we should walk in them"*
> *(Eph. 2:10).*

Randall's story is an incredible testimony to the power of brief encounters. It also shows that God has purpose for every life. Randall and Mr. James only worked together for a couple months, and the amount of times they were able to talk was far fewer. Four years after their conversation, Mr. James died from cancer, but not before Randall was able to tell him how he changed his life.

We do not know Mr. James's story or how many lives he touched outside of Randall's, but look at the beauty that has come from this one interaction in his life. At some point, Mr. James accepted God into his life, which impacted Randall opening his life up to God. This impact trickled on to Randall's friends and brother, all of whom have impacted others' lives and will continue to impact lives for years to come.

God does not waste time or lives. He did not create us just to exist. He created us to thrive and prosper. He created us to be messengers of his love and redemption. He has given each of us an innate gift that is to be used to help bring others to Him. He created each of us with a purpose all our own—a purpose that will be fulfilled when we open our hearts and cry out to him, "God, I want to live my life for You!"

Chapter Two
Changing Your Mind-Set

For the last six years or so, I have been an unabashed optimist. I tend to look at the ups and downs of life and try to figure out how they are bettering me as a person or to interpret what God is trying to teach me. When a friend or family member comes to me with a problem, I do the same thing. I try to point out the positive even in the worst of situations or bring to light how God is working in their life. I have learned though that with unabashed optimism comes the need to be aware of when to incorporate empathy.

I was not always an unabashed optimist. Not that I was ever really a pessimist. I guess I would have called myself a realist. I was a glass half full with a side of "this is how it is, and that's it." For the majority of my life, I didn't necessarily seek out the silver-lining to my problems. I would just work to overcome them on my own, and not worry about the consequences of how I handled the trials. I lived on a positive–negative teeter totter trying to balance at neutral, and it was exhausting.

I want you to look at the scenarios below and think about which one you fall under.

Scenario 1:

I do not fear the things of the world, because I know God is in control. If I am willing to do the work, God will continue to provide blessing after blessing. The trials of this life are God's way of preparing me for future blessings. During my trials, I know God is with me. God has a purpose for me. I understand that even if I feel ready, I must not get frustrated if things are not working out yet, because that means God is working on others to make my journey easier. No matter what happens in my life, good or bad, I will continue to praise and worship Him.

Scenario 2:

Nothing ever works out when it should. That's just my luck. I feel like God doesn't hear my prayers or I don't pray at all. I wish life was easier. I feel like nothing ever goes right. Every plan I make falls through. I can get through my trials on my own. I often don't think about God whether my life is going in a positive or negative direction.

Scenario 3:

Somewhere in between scenarios 1 and 2. I believe God loves me and wants the best for me, but there are times I question His intentions. I try to be patient with His timing, but often get frustrated when things don't work out when I want them to. I talk about how great God is when life is good, but when I face trials, I find it hard to praise Him.

For those of you that fall under scenario 2 or 3, do not look down upon yourself or feel inadequate. Being a scenario-2 or -3 person does not make you a bad person. It makes you a person who is at a different level in their walk with God, but you have every capability to have scenario 1 kind of faith. God understands where you are in your walk and loves you just the same. He wants better for you though. He wants you to know in the very depths of your soul that He is watching over you, and no matter your situation it will work out for the best. You make the choice though as to how open you want to be to God's love and mercy.

> "Do not worry at all, but in every matter, by prayer and petition, with thanksgiving, let your requests be made known to Elohim. And the peace of Elohim, which surpasses all understanding, shall guard your hearts and minds through Messiah Yeshua" (Phil. 4:6–7).

The action that moves you from scenario to scenario is a change in your mind-set. When you constantly think negatively about your life, your life will be negative. You won't see the everyday small blessings that God has given you. You may not even see the in-your-face miracles God is working in your life. Negativity breeds negativity. Click off the repeat button on your negative thoughts. Start training your brain to think positively. Do you know who you can seek to help retrain your brain? You guessed it—God. If you are tired of living a negative lifestyle, go to Him and ask for help. He can help you change your mind-set in the blink of an eye.

Just like negativity breeds negativity, positivity will breed positivity. I genuinely cannot turn off the part of my brain that always looks for the miracle in the midst of the chaos. I have watched things crumble around me and known that something great was going to come of the rubble. When you keep a positive mind-set, you can't help but see God's work in your life.

The impact God has in your life is in direct correlation to your mind-set. When you praise God and are willing to work with Him in the blessings he provides you, He will make His love, mercy and grace abundantly present. When you praise you are not igno-rant to the trials you face, you are proclaiming that no trial, no matter how big, is above God's reach. Fully accepting God as the authority over your life, refraining from the knee-jerk reaction to act negatively to trials, opens up blessings and a peace that can only be of God. Do you want to be a praise giver or a spiri-tual pauper?

Sam

> *"And we had to rejoice and be glad, for your brother*
> *was dead and is alive, and was lost and is found"*
> *(Luke 15:32).*

When I say meeting Sam was divinely guided, I am not exag-gerating. For three years, my oldest daughter was in an art class at a locally owned craft studio. One day (about two years into her time there), I took her and our middle daughter to a mommy and me class. It was at that class that I re-met Sam's wife, Brittany. I say we re-met because Brittany and I went to high school together, but we didn't hang out in the same crowds. So when we sat near each other in the mommy and me class, we recognized each other and realized that we had known each other over a decade ago. I also found out that they homeschooled, like us, which was very exciting to me, but that was the extent of the conversation. We didn't connect on social media. We just talked, and that was it.

A year later, my oldest, who had just reached the age for kin-dergarten, got moved up to the first–third grade art class. Guess who was in the class? Brittany and Sam's oldest daughter, who was in first grade at the time. Our two oldest became best friends. When I say best friends, I mean so much so that every time they saw each other before art it was like something out of the movies.

They would both run to each other with arms wide open and give each other the biggest hug. It was adorable.

So, of course, since both girls are homeschooled and now the "bestest friends ever," Brittany and I started having play dates with our kids. Eventually we brought our husbands around, and everyone became friends.

It was fifteen years from the time Brittany and I were in high school together to all of us becoming friends. God worked for over a decade on all of us adults, culminating in our two oldest daughters, ages five and six, being the ones that solidified the work God had been doing to bring us all together. This is why I say meeting Sam (and Brittany) was divinely guided. God knew I would be writing this book, and he knew Sam was supposed to share his story.

Sam's memories of his childhood are not filled with many of the typical childhood memories: playing with neighborhood friends, new toys at Christmas, innocence. Sam's memories are of being incredibly poor living in a trailer park and not having electricity in the winter in Indiana. His Christmas presents were getting his toys out of the pawn shop, and knowing if he went outside the trailer, he was going to have to fight someone. Being around alcoholism, weed, and verbal abuse were the norm for him. While his dad lashed out frequently, he made sure his kids kept on the right line as Sam's cousins went to prison at a young age.

Sam's mom's side of the family were devout Catholics. His Grandma gave him a rosary when he was young. Every time he would come over, she was always cooking Spanish food, and despite living in poverty, her yard was always perfect when all the other neighbor's yards were trashy. The only time Sam went to church was for Christmas and Easter. He believed in God but didn't know much, past what he heard those two days a year.

With the examples before him, Sam knew he never wanted to be like what he saw regularly. He didn't want to go to jail like his cousins, and he wanted to give his kids a better life than what he had.

When Sam was eleven, his dad was facing thirty years in prison on kidnapping charges related to a drug deal that had gone bad. A friend of Sam's dad had broken protocol when it came to getting drugs, and in the process, he lost money. The friend wasn't happy about it and took one of the dealers—who was part of a gang—"for a ride" with Sam's dad. The gang member jumped out of the car while they were driving. Sam's dad and his friend were arrested for kidnapping. Both Sam's dad and the friend got probation. The drug dealers still weren't happy with Sam's dad though. Sam's parent's house was shot at, and a .38 slug hit next to the car seat his little brother was sitting in. That was a turning point for his dad. Sam's dad knew they had to get out of Indiana. Once his probation was completed, they moved to Florida. The friend of Sam's dad that had been involved in the kidnapping paid for them to move to Florida, where he was already living. This man became like an uncle to Sam, and his son like a cousin.

When they moved to Florida, church no longer was a part of the family's life, even on Christmas and Easter. They had one Bible in the house, but it was never opened. Sam was shown Revelations at one point, but nothing soaked in. Sam even went to church at fourteen to become the godfather of his second cousin, but he did not retain anything then either. He enjoyed walking and hearing the bells, but when it came to the teachings, he just went through the motions.

At sixteen, Sam became involved with a toxic group of friends through his cousin who was two years older. Sam began to drink and do drugs. At first the drugs were Xanax and weed, but he progressed to using Ecstasy. Ecstasy was like the devil consuming him. Sam would spend two weeks not knowing what day it was. He was in a constant euphoric state that opened the door to a lot of crazy.

Sam's cousin, albeit older, had cerebral palsy. His cousin didn't let it stop him from living his life though. He had trouble walking but was still on the high school basketball team. Even though he didn't let his disabilities stop him, others still made fun of him. There was one particular bully at school that was taking it too far and getting physically aggressive with Sam's cousin.

One day Sam got a call from his "aunt" telling him about the bullying his cousin was receiving. Sam was a freshman. The bully was a senior, but Sam wasn't going to let him treat his cousin like that. Sam and the senior got into a fight at school that day. There were no cameras where they were fighting. However, Sam still ended up getting a felony battery charge. Sam would spend almost three years in and out of court, eventually receiving a hundred hours community service.

It was around this time that Sam began to realize that his "uncle and cousin" came from a very violent family. It was also around that time that Sam's dad realized that his friend, who was like an uncle to Sam, was giving Sam weed. His dad was incredibly mad that his friend was enabling Sam. The friendship ended shortly thereafter.

"Do not be wise in your own eyes; fear Yahweh and turn away from evil" (Prov. 3:7).

When Sam was sixteen, his grandpa got out of jail. He had been in jail most of Sam's life. Sam's grandpa was also an alcoholic and smoked weed. Even though Sam didn't know his grandpa for most of his life, they began to connect once he was out of jail. One thing that drew Sam to his grandpa was that he could recite Bible verses without hesitation. Unfortunately, their relationship would not last long, because his grandpa died about a year after he was released from jail. That loss led Sam down a very dark path.

God would use this loss to bring someone else into Sam's life. Sam met Brittany when he was eighteen. Brittany knew about his grandpa and Sam's lifestyle. When he was in a dark place, he would call Brittany to come get him. Sometimes she would do drugs with him, but there were many times he would ask her to come over and bring drugs and she would show up without them.

There were times that Sam would play Brittany by bringing other girls to parties she was at. He knew Brittany wanted to make it work, but at the same time she wasn't going to be treated like a fool. She made that known to him too. She would eventually share news with him that would force him to begin to make changes.

Brittany was pregnant with their child. Initially, Sam and Brittany were unsure as to whether they should keep the baby or not. They received support for both keeping the baby and aborting the baby which caused confusion. After much thought, Brittany decided she was going to keep the baby. Some heated discussions occurred during this time about their future. However, Sam and Brittany realized that they were in this together and would move forward as a family.

The news of her pregnancy did not change Sam's opinion on partying at first. Brittany would go to the parties with him, but she would flush any drugs that were given to her and not drink. Sam, however, was on a total path of destruction, but then he found out they were having a girl.

He said, "What am I going to do with two of you?" He knew he had to start getting his act together. He continued to drink and smoke weed but quit everything else.

When they had their daughter, Sam felt a sense of normality for the first time in a long time. He was happy. His daughter had his whole heart. Sam also started getting things lined up so he could take better care of his family. Sam and Brittany were married shortly after their daughter was born.

After his daughter was born, Sam went to HVAC school. He and his family moved out of his parent's lanai as well. It was hard for Sam to leave his parents, because he helped pay the bills. He knew that if he left that would make things harder on his mom. However, he knew he had a family and especially a baby that he needed to take care of. Sam and his family would move in with Brittany's family for a short period of time before renting an apartment, and eventually being able to buy their first home.

Two years after their daughter was born, Brittany and Sam found out they were going to have another child. This time the baby was going to be a boy: Samuel Jr. Sam and Brittany were very excited to be adding to their family. The pregnancy seemed fairly routine until a couple weeks before Brittany was due. One-night Brittany told Sam that something didn't seem right. She couldn't feel the baby moving like she should. Sam dismissed her concerns. They had already had one child with no complications, so he didn't think there would be any complications this time, especially since they were only a couple weeks from their due date. Sam chose that night to get drunk instead.

The next day, Sam left for work and went about his day like any other day. In the afternoon, Sam got a call saying he needed to come to the hospital. Sam was excited because he thought Brittany had gone into labor and was having their son. He remembered that the song "Sinners Like Me," by Eric Church, was playing on the radio on the way to the hospital. When Sam walked into the hospital room, he saw Brittany sitting in the hospital bed completely stone-faced. She turned to him and told him that she lost the baby. Samuel Jr. had died in utero. Brittany had to deliver their "sleeping" son now.

> *"Yahweh is near to the broken-hearted, and saves those whose spirit is crushed" (Ps. 34:18).*

When Sam got to hold his son, he was wrecked with the what-ifs, and he felt immense guilt for not taking Brittany to the hospital when she had first asked him to. He began to question God. Why had God not taken him? Sam cried a lot the day he lost his son, and like the night before, he got drunk.

Sam and Brittany would eventually go back to their life at home. Sam saw Brittany displaying the strength he always knew she had taking care of everyone even during her time of mourning. It was at this time though that Sam started going down a dark path alone that he had never been down before.

There were two ways Sam was able to get drugs easily: working in construction and taking prescription drugs. Getting drugs while in construction was easy. They called them "power-ups." Sam started out getting two at a time, eventually buying fifteen at one time. Once, Sam was driving with his daughter in the car and thought about the fact that he was driving with felonies in his pocket. Sam also got into a bad car accident. The car had burned to the ground. The only way he escaped was by cutting his seatbelt. Due to the pain from the accident, the doctor prescribed him Vicodin. Sam didn't take the Vicodin for pain. Sam would take two Vicodin at a time recreationally to get high. Since he was in such a bad car accident, he could go to the emergency room claiming pain, and they would give him more.

The two years following his son's death were very rough for Sam. Brittany didn't show any grief for a long time, and that scared Sam. He was concerned about what she may do, and at the same time did not want her to have his grief to add on to her life. He didn't want Brittany to worry about him, so he didn't tell her about any of his addictions or what he was going through. Sam could tell Brittany was questioning his use of Vicodin, because of comments she would make, but they never discussed it. Sam began to consume lots of alcohol as well. Jim Beam became a regular drink of choice on the weekends.

While Sam was personally in a dark place, he didn't let that get in the way of his relationship with his daughter. He never shunned her, and really enjoyed his time with her. He made sure to still have fun with her taking her for rides in the truck around the woods on their property, going mudding, getting a dog together, and spending plenty of time outside playing. He still remembered that he didn't want his daughter to go through what he did as a child.

And then there was a rainbow. Sam was so happy when he found out they would be welcoming their third child but was also very worried. It was a positive step in their lives, but every time Brittany had a doctor's appointment, Sam would be anxious to hear the report. Sam and Brittany welcomed the birth of their second daughter, their rainbow baby, two years after their son's passing. Sam was very glad to have another daughter. He was also thankful for her birth for both Brittany and their oldest daughter. Even though it had been years since their son's passing and they had another beautiful daughter, Sam was still doing drugs secretly. However, now he started to actually struggle with his choice to take drugs. He had two daughters now that depended on him. He needed to get his act together.

However, Sam was still fighting the guilt and pain of losing his son. He would often go out to his shed, sit at the table with weed and his 9mm gun, and fantasize about killing himself. The fantasizing led to him putting the gun in his mouth, but he knew he could never do it. "I knew Brittany was strong and could take care of herself, but I couldn't leave my daughters like that." Sam began to claw his way out of the darkness. Sitting in front of his weed and gun, he made the decision to flush the weed, and to never point the gun at himself again.

On a whim, Sam went to a church after a really bad day at work. Sam had called the suicide hotline before, and it had never been much help. He wanted to talk to someone in person. He drove to a church he had been to a couple times and knocked on the door. He told the person who came to the door that he needed to talk to someone about God. They wouldn't let him in. The woman seemed annoyed that Sam was even there. She told him they couldn't help him at the time as they were all inside praying. He then asked them if he could come in and get a drink. He figured that if they let him in to get a drink from the water fountain that was near the door, then he could walk around until he found someone who was willing to listen. She didn't let him in for a drink either. Now this was during a time when there had been quite a few church shootings, so he figured that was why they hesitated, but he was still upset by the fact that he couldn't speak to someone to receive counseling. Despite the woman's actions Sam went home and flushed all the pills he had. He had had enough of his addiction. While Sam would not receive the counseling, he needed from a church, God heard Sam's plea for help, and was guiding him to what he needed in order to make a change.

> *"And if we know that He hears us, whatever we ask,*
> *we know that we have the petitions that we have*
> *asked of Him" (1 John 5:15).*

In 2018, four years after Sam's son had passed, Sam's life would be changed in an unexpected way. Sam went to a work convention with Brittany. One of the main speakers was a gentleman who had worked his way up through the company. The man talked about growing up with a broke-mind-set. The speaker explained how he was constantly living in fear and acknowledging that he didn't have enough or that he would run out of money. The speaker said that it was a fundamental fear of loss/being without. He also talked about how he overcame that mind-set. Sam could relate to the man's past and saw potential for his future. Sam realized if this man speaking could make a change then he could too.

Sam's mind-set began to change. During that convention, God gave Sam a vision for his future. Sam clung to it but knew he would have to tread through water to get to it. Brittany began sending him personal development podcasts that she was listening to grow her business. Sam would go out to the shed at night and pour over the podcasts. Initially Sam would still smoke weed while listening to the podcasts, but then he began to get frustrated with the fact he couldn't keep up with what the podcasts were discussing. Sam got rid of all the weed and focused on personal development.

> *"If, then, the Son makes you free, you shall be free indeed" (John 8:36).*

During this time of clarity and growth, Sam and Brittany began trying out different churches with varying denominations, but none felt right. After a few months of trying out new churches, Brittany got a message from one of her friends that she had started going to a new church. The reason their friend started going to that particular church was because they had a dream that they went to the church, and Brittany was there welcoming people as they walked into the church.

Sam and Brittany took that as a sign they should check out the church with their friend. Sam was impressed with the church but wasn't sure how to take it. However, when he saw how excited his daughters were coming out of the youth service, he knew they had to come back. Sam also began to feel eager to go to church again, and for the first time opened his Bible to truly read it.

Sam and his family returned to the church the following week. After leaving service, Sam's youngest daughter began to tell him about the scripture they were learning in their class. It was the same scripture that Sam had been reading before coming to church that day. Sam was amazed.

He called Brittany's grandpa. He asked, "Have you ever had things align?" Brittany's grandpa replied that with God in his life things aligned all the time. Sam was so excited. He began digging into the word regularly.

The way Sam looked at his life began to change. Sam began to recognize the chains that held his family back. He began talking with God, and calling his dad quoting scripture. He brought both his parents to church, and they each received a message that they connected with. Sam found himself talking about God whenever possible. One night after reading the Bible, Sam put the Bible on his nightstand and laid there in bed. All of a sudden, he felt the Holy Spirit come over him. He felt like he was floating off the bed and had electricity going through him. He felt calm, but slightly overwhelmed. He couldn't go back to bed after that happened. It was like nothing Sam had ever experienced before. He was incredibly happy.

"But all matters being convicted are manifested by the light, for whatever is manifested is light. That

is why He says, "Wake up, you who sleep, and arise from the dead, and Messiah shall shine on you." See then that you walk exactly, not as unwise, but as wise, redeeming the time because the days are wicked" (Eph. 5:13–16).

How Sam viewed trials in his life also changed. Sam was no longer getting angry when trials occurred. He adopted a no-problem attitude. "You can't stop the blessings of God." During this time of spiritual growth, Sam and Brittany were facing challenges within their jobs.

Sam had the vision for opening a nutrition club, but things were not aligning like they had planned. With one contract falling through, things were getting tight for them. However, just when they needed it the most, an opportunity presented itself: an excellent location with reasonable rent. Sam and Brittany were able to open their nutrition club. Even with the minor setbacks, Sam knew that God would provide for them, and provide He has. Since opening their club, many people come in and tell Sam that they felt like they had to come there. Their conversation will continue, and Sam will use that opportunity to share the Word with them. Sam and Brittany have seen exponential growth in less than a year of opening their nutrition club. Sam believes God gave Brittany and him a platform to speak and share His word.

Sam has also felt past hurts relieved once he connected with God. He felt as if he was covered in mud: unclean and unworthy. However, he now feels washed clean by the Word. Sam is at peace with his son's passing, and no longer feels the pain or guilt he once did. Sam realized he had the choice to still be happy. God helped him to choose happiness, and Sam honors God's gift of peace through sharing His word. "God has blessed me beyond physical understanding."

"These words I have spoken to you, that in Me you might have peace. In the world you have pressure, but take courage, I have overcome the world" (John 16:33).

Sam has also taken the opportunity to serve at the church in the youth ministry. His first time in the youth service Sam was blown away by their innocence. The kids worshipped without caring about what other kids thought. He was amazed to see over time how much the kids would grow spiritually. Initially starting as a helper, Sam has now preached at one of the youth services.

"I say to you, in the same way there is joy in the presence of the messengers of Elohim over one sinner repenting" (Luke 15:10).

Sam's life was completely transformed when he accepted God into his life and allowed God to change his mind-set. Sam went from "Scenario 2: Nothing ever works out when it should... I feel like God doesn't hear my prayers or I don't pray at all. I wish life was easier... I can get through my trials on my own. I often don't think about God whether my life is going in a positive or negative direction" to "Scenario 1: I do not fear the things of the world because I know God is in control. If I am willing to do the work, God will continue to provide blessing after blessing. The trials of this life are God's way of preparing me for future blessings. During my trials, I know God is with me... No matter what happens in my life, good or bad, I will continue to praise and worship Him."

Sam felt peace in the midst of heartbreaking pain. His eyes were opened to spirits (chains) he had yet to see/accept. He gained strength and clarity in his actions. He was baptized in the Holy Spirit and shares the Word with others regularly. Sam's outlook is perpetually positive even in the face of adversity. His life was forever changed when he realized he could change this mind-set and allowed God to guide him.

Chapter Three
Allow God to Guide You

It was a life-altering moment when my husband said he wanted to become a farmer. Neither of us had ever lived on a farm or worked with livestock. I knew that the months my husband had spent researching agriculture, listening to podcasts, and attending farming conventions wasn't just for fun. I knew this conversation was coming. Yet somehow, I still wasn't fully prepared for what was in store for us.

My husband's farming dreams came true the day we brought home twenty-seven Florida Cracker sheep in January of 2014. The first year was a very uncertain time filled with lots of on-the-job learning especially on my part. The ironic thing here though is he was still working full-time so it was left to me and our almost one year old to tend to the sheep for the most part. Never had I ever dreamed I would be tending to livestock. Although, I was excited to have sheep because they were cute and very relaxing to watch.

We decided to do what is called rotational grazing, which means the sheep are kept in one paddock for the day and then moved to the next paddock on the next day. This allows the sheep to always have fresh grass, eliminates a lot of parasite problems and gives our field time to rest. To do these daily moves we used electric fencing. The sheep learned very quickly not to touch it, or they got shocked. (Don't worry, it's like static electricity.) It startles them way more than it is painful. Every lambing season, the lambs have to learn about the fences and being moved paddock to paddock.

During our first lambing season I felt like I joined the rodeo every time I moved the sheep. There was always one lamb that wouldn't pay attention when we were moving paddocks. The mom and the rest of the flock would leave it behind because they were excited about new grass. (I'll give the mom some credit though she would baa for the baby as she was running into the next paddock.) The lamb would run back and forth along the fence line trying to figure out how to get to the flock even though there was a ten-foot section missing from the fence that the rest of the flock ran through. All it saw though was the fence it knew it shouldn't touch and on the other side was where it was supposed to be.

It was now up to me, a complete farm animal novice, to wrangle this incredibly spry little lamb into the next paddock. The amount of times I slid on and fell into sheep poop to help a lamb are far too numerous to count. I smelled. I was sweaty because let's face it springtime in Florida may as well be summer, but I always made sure the lamb got back with the flock.

I wasn't worried about the rest of the flock. I knew they were okay because we had electric fencing protecting them from outside predators, and they were chowing down on fresh grass. I also knew this lamb needed my help even if it didn't act like it. It needed to be guided to the place it was supposed to be. After about two weeks, the lamb finally got the hang of the moves, and I didn't have to get my cardio in while moving the sheep—until the next lambing season and another lamb did the same thing. By the second year of farming, I had gained a lot more patience and knowledge so things went a lot smoother.

*"What do you think? If a man has a hundred sheep,
and one of them goes astray, would he not leave
the ninety-nine on the mountains, going to seek
the one that is straying? And if he should find it,
truly, I say to you, he rejoices more over that sheep
than over the ninety-nine that did not go astray"
(Matt. 18:12–13).*

God is your Shepherd. God will find you when you have lost your way and take care of you. He will protect you and bring you to where you need to be. Unlike myself in our first year of farming, He is not a novice. He has seen it all and knows all to come. He knows what incredible things lie ahead of you.

*"Great is our Master and mighty in power, there is
no limit to His understanding" (Ps. 147:5).*

Like the lamb, you need to be willing to listen. You need to stop your dodging and weaving and take a moment to listen to what he is telling/showing you. You see all my poop sliding did was scare the lamb more which frustrated me. It was a vicious cycle. It wasn't until I stopped chasing it, let it calm down, and assess its situation that I was able to guide it into the next paddock. The lamb realized, "Oh, hey, there is this big gap where there is no longer a barrier." It slowly started to walk toward the gap I had left for it. I would still walk behind it to make sure it didn't get spooked at the last moment and turn back around again. God wants to take you to the next step in your story. He wants to take you to the greener grass. He will speak to you and guide you. If you get spooked, he will be there when you turn around and show you that he is still watching over you.

Rachel

"'For I know the plans I am planning for you'
declares Yahweh, 'plans of peace and not of evil, to
give you a future and an expectancy'" (Jer. 29:11).

October 2019 was the first time I saw Rachel. Our family had just started attending the church we attend now, and I noticed her praising at the altar during the worship portion of the service. I could tell the music was having a big impact on her. Her emotions were easy to see, and I couldn't help but think she must have overcome a lot to be praising so hard. When God told me to write the book, she was the first person I thought to ask even though I had only spoken to her a couple times prior. She was my first interview, and the first person who gave me a glimpse into how powerful this book was going to be.

For many years, Rachel's father was involved in ministry. While they were initially Baptist, Rachel's parents became Pentecostal. Rachel's father received an education in ministry, after which he became an ordained minister. Once he graduated, the family moved to Wisconsin where he became an intern at a large church and began to learn about church planting. While he was still an intern, he and Rachel's mother joined a stateside missionary organization. This missionary organization sent Rachel's dad and family to Kansas to help a church that at the time was not willing to receive help. Rachel remembers her dad enjoying his work as a pastor while they lived in Kansas, but he was struggling mentally and emotionally. Rachel remembers that when her father took the position he seemed to be disheartened. The church they were a part of did not allow emotion. Losing that aspect of his preaching was very hard on her father.

While he had a Christian foundation, there were some aspects that he did not follow that caused a strain on his relationship with Rachel's mother, Rachel, and her younger brothers. Rachel's dad was an adulterer. When Rachel was thirteen, she caught her father in a relationship with her best friend's mom. It made Rachel angry to see her dad treat her mom that way, especially since he would flirt with the woman, he was having extramarital relations with in front of Rachel's mom.

Rachel's dad was also physically abusive to Rachel's middle brother and verbally abusive to Rachel. Rachel's family believed her father suffered from bipolar depression. He would have months of manic high's where he would buy the kids things like a puppy, which was very out of character. As far up as he would go, he would also swing deep down. The puppy he bought he got rid of without explanation. He became aggressive, abusive, and suicidal. Rachel remembers hearing her mother and father talking, and her mother telling him, "If you are going to commit suicide, wait until I'm with family."

When Rachel's parents realized living in Kansas was no longer good for them, they moved back to California. Rachel's dad took a job as a handyman. Once he became a handyman, Rachel doesn't really remember her dad being home much due to long work hours, and him regularly attending the gym. However, he would make sure they still attended church on Wednesdays and Sundays. Moving to California also showed Rachel a side of her father that hurt her.

It became apparent to Rachel that her dad was not going to make an effort to have a relationship with her when he was home. She tried to do things to make him proud, and to hear that he loved her. He never acknowledged her accomplishments.

Two years after moving back to California, Rachel's father committed suicide. This rocked Rachel's family. She was only thirteen, and she had two younger brothers. Their dad was gone, and their mother became reclusive. Rachel was sad and upset for her mom and brothers, but she would not mourn long for her father. She allowed herself one night to grieve, and then shut it off. Rachel used her independent nature and strength to get her through the trauma and help her mom and brothers. The year her father died everything became a blur. Rachel's family stopped going to church. She knew it was wrong of her to leave the church but didn't feel convicted about it enough to change her mind.

When their father died, Rachel's middle brother (the one their father physically abused) snapped. Like his dad, Rachel's middle brother started showing signs of bipolar depression. During his manic low moments, he became very violent toward Rachel. Rachel's mother was concerned that he may hurt Rachel if one of their fights went too far.

Rachel was also going through her own teen angst. She was not home much, spending time at friend's houses and was very disrespectful to her mother when she was home. Rachel was also suicidal. When Rachel was fifteen, she was sent to Northern California to live with her aunt.

Looking back on it now, Rachel recognizes that was the best thing her mom could have ever done for her. Rachel's aunt was very different from her mother. Her aunt was structured. She had routines including attending church regularly. Rachel's aunt also wasn't afraid to put her in her place when Rachel acted out but in a Christian way and not abusive. Rachel was able to find her relationship with God, and this time it stuck because she chose it. God took hold of her and she became on fire for God. After a year living with her aunt, Rachel would have to go home. She didn't want to leave, because she had the structure and discipline she needed, but she had to go. Her mom had chosen to move to Southern California which was too far from her aunt, and her mom wanted her to be at home.

When Rachel moved back in with her family, things were very different than when she had left. Her mother had moved to a house that needed extensive remodeling on ten acres in the middle of the southern hills of California. They did not have a functional kitchen. Tarantulas, scorpions, snakes, and other unwanted creatures would come into the house. Rachel, on occasion, would find her bed covered in centipedes. Her youngest brother was now living with their grandma. Her middle brother was stable and medicated. However, Rachel's mother had become catatonic. Rachel had to give her medication, food and take her to the bathroom. Rachel tried to go to school, but she quickly began failing her classes. Rachel dropped out of high school her sophomore year because she was falling behind in her classes. It also made it easier to take care of her mom if she wasn't going to school. During this time Rachel relied on God a lot to get her from day to day.

> *"Without guidance the people fall, but in a great counsellor there is safety" (Prov. 11:14).*

God was with Rachel as she tried to help her mom. One day, Rachel was playing a Reliant K CD while she was taking a shower. She heard God say to her, "This will pull her out." She knew He was talking about her mom so as quickly as she could she took the CD player outside for her mom to listen to the song. As she watched her mom listen to the song, Rachel could see the light come back into her mother's eyes. Her mother came back from her numb, unresponsive state. Rachel's mom had felt like God had left her. The song reminded Rachel's mom that God loved her and that He was there for her. It pulled Rachel's mom out of her sorrow, and back to life. Within weeks Rachel's mother was working again, and they found a church to go to. Seeing her mother's transformation proved to Rachel, without a shadow of a doubt, that God loved them. While Rachel's mom was being pulled out of darkness, Rachel was getting ready to experience a darkness she had not yet been exposed to.

At sixteen, Rachel met a man on the internet, whom she thought she loved, and she thought he loved her too. She was excited because he said he was saved, and she thought she had found someone who would share her love for God. He would spend the weekend's at Rachel's house, and she lost her virginity to him. It was during his weekend stays he began to become verbally abusive. Despite the verbal abuse, Rachel married him on her eighteenth birthday. Shortly after their marriage, they moved to Florida with Rachel's mom and brothers. This move would not last long though for Rachel and her new husband. Six months after moving to Florida, Rachel and her husband moved to Las Vegas to live with his father. It was at this time she started to notice his behavior worsening.

Rachel's husband became incredibly manipulative and verbally abusive. He began to call her worthless, ugly, and many other bad names. Yet, while he was calling her these names, he was also telling her that no one would ever love her like he did. Not only did he speak to Rachel horribly, he also physically abused her. He would drag Rachel through the house by her hair and put her in chokeholds. While he would never hit her, he would use his body weight to overpower her and rape her on several occasions. While Rachel wasn't happy, she continued to stay with him out of guilt. She wanted to try to make the marriage work.

Almost a year into their marriage, Rachel's husband and his father decided to go on a vacation to the Philippines. Upon their return, Rachel got incredibly sick. She could not move or take care of herself. She had never been in so much pain in her life. Her husband grew tired of taking care of her. He put her in the bathtub and filled it with water. He left her there for two or three days without checking on her. By this point Rachel was going in and out of consciousness. Eventually, Rachel's father-in-law, who worked nights as a correctional officer, asked his son where Rachel was. That's when Rachel's husband told him that she was sick, and she had been in the tub for a few days. Rachel remembers her father-in-law making her husband take her out of the bathroom. Rachel's husband grabbed her out of the tub and forced her to dress herself even though she could barely stand. Both Rachel's father-in-law and husband took her to the hospital.

Rachel had a 106.9 fever, her organs were failing, and her body had become septic. The doctors could not figure out what she had even after exploratory abdominal surgery and multiple blood draws. On the fourth day in the hospital, Rachel went into cardiac arrest. She saw the code blue light and woke up in a different place.

Rachel was in a white room with marble floors. The bed she was sitting in had marble columns and was the most comfortable bed she had ever been in. In the corner of the room, Rachel saw a white tiger. (Tigers are her favorite animals.) She felt like a kid, and she had immense peace. The room was very bright. As she looked around, she heard a voice speak to her. "You can't stay here. It's not time for you to stay here yet. You need to go back. Go back to sleep." Rachel put her head on the pillow and woke up in the hospital.

> *"And you, you intended evil against me, but Elohim*
> *intended it for good, in order to do it as it is this day,*
> *to keep a great many people alive" (Gen. 50:20).*

From that moment, Rachel began to recover. However, due to the trauma from the illness and extreme loss in strength/weight,

Rachel had to receive physical therapy while in the hospital. She didn't let that stop her from living her life, though. Rachel was back at work one week after she got out of the hospital. Rachel fully recovered within three weeks. She was able to save up enough money to move to Florida and divorced her husband by the age of nineteen. She was finally happy, had peace and was not sick anymore.

By twenty, Rachel had met another man. This time she became pregnant with her daughter. This man was different from her ex-husband. He wasn't abusive, but he was neglectful, drank and did drugs. He didn't want a relationship with Rachel but felt like he should because he had gotten her pregnant.

Shortly before Rachel's daughter was born, they moved to Maine to be closer to his family. Rachel agreed, but had some concerns. As soon as she stepped off the bus in Maine, Rachel knew she had made a bad choice. Yet again, she felt trapped and did not have the money to get back home. About a month after their move, Rachel's boyfriend decided that he no longer wanted to be with her, but he also didn't want their daughter to be around her either.

Rachel was at home with her one-week old daughter when she heard a knock on the door. A woman from DCF was there on an anonymous tip that Rachel had been shaking her daughter. Rachel was floored, but since she didn't have anything to hide, she allowed the DCF worker to come in and question her. Rachel was asked if she remembered ever shaking her baby. She responded "No, I do not remember ever shaking my baby." The woman used those words to say that Rachel was not fit to be a mother because she "could not remember ever shaking her baby." Rachel was horrified. She had never shaken her baby and thought she had answered the question properly to prove that. Rachel's daughter at one week old was taken from her. Having her daughter taken from her was like mourning the death of her child but knowing she was not dead.

The parents of Rachel's boyfriend were granted temporary custody of Rachel's daughter. Rachel was only allowed supervised visits to see her daughter four hours a day. She wasn't allowed to breastfeed her daughter either, so she had to let herself dry up. This devastated Rachel. Not only had she had her daughter taken from her, she had also lost the ability to create those bonding moments when she did see her. It was about to get even worse. She was soon told she was no longer allowed to see her daughter. Rachel knew she had to fight this. Her daughter was precious to her, and she did not want to lose her.

Rachel's grandparents paid for her lawyer, but Rachel had to make the incredibly difficult choice to leave her daughter and move back to Florida. For two years, Rachel fought for her daughter. She had to prove she had stable income, housing, and support to raise a child. She also had to prove her ex's inability to care for their child which wasn't difficult as he had a substance abuse problem, did not hold a steady job or have steady housing. The best words she ever heard were "granting full custody."

Getting full custody of her daughter would raise challenges Rachel wasn't expecting. Rachel and her daughter did not have a relationship. Rachel's new boyfriend did not want her holding her daughter constantly and didn't want Rachel to bottle feed her. He felt like Rachel was going to spoil her daughter. Rachel felt robbed of the first milestones and sad that she couldn't connect with her daughter better. However, this feeling wouldn't last forever. When her daughter turned five, their bond became established.

When Rachel's daughter was three, Rachel became pregnant again with her boyfriend that didn't want her holding her first daughter too much. He was the first guy Rachel really loved, but looking back, she doesn't think he really loved her. Sadly, this pregnancy would end in a miscarriage, and end their relationship.

Shortly after the loss of her second child, Rachel moved back in with her mother. Rachel began going back to church. Her life began getting back on track. She was on fire for God again and was thoroughly enjoying motherhood. As she began to grow in her faith, she met another man. This man was substantially older than Rachel. He was forty-five, and she was twenty-seven. She was not attracted to him at all, but he said he loved God and wanted to serve Him. Rachel was excited to meet a man who aligned with her love for God.

A couple months after meeting they got married. Rachel moved her and her daughter in with her second husband at his mom's house. They were together for two years before Rachel found out that they were not legally married. When Rachel found out they weren't legally married, she was upset, but she did not let it get in the way of their relationship. It was also during this time he had started to become verbally and physically abusive. Much like her other exes he convinced her to stay despite the abuse. Rachel also found out that she was pregnant with his child. This time they got legally married and their own place. However, the abuse would become more frequent and started becoming sadistic.

When Rachel went in for her six-week checkup, she was told they couldn't find the baby's heartbeat, and that they would have to do an intrauterine ultrasound. They still couldn't find a heartbeat. At eight weeks, Rachel miscarried her third child. Unlike the first miscarriage, Rachel felt excruciating pain. This was the second child she lost. Rachel felt broken. She felt like less of a woman. She battled with knowing she could get pregnant, but that two out of three had not been carried to term. Shortly after her miscarriage, her second marriage ended.

*"On me, O Elohim, are Your vows; I render praises
to You, for You have delivered my life from death,
my feet from stumbling, that I might walk before
Elohim, in the light of the living!" (Ps. 56:12–13).*

In fewer than thirty years, Rachel had been through the gauntlet between domestic violence, losing her daughter for two years, and having two miscarriages. During this time though she did not lose her faith. She was able to keep her faith through her music. From twelve years old to present, Rachel would write songs to express what she was going through. Each song, even if it wasn't Christian based, incorporated faith. She had the foundation, and never felt completely alone. There were times she felt guilty for straying and was scared to come back to God. However, she knew the fear she had was the devil at work. Once she learned there was no condemnation in Christ, she was relieved of her fear. She knew that no matter what her physical hurt was, God did not want that. Little did she know that God was getting ready to make a big move in her life.

Eventually, Rachel would make her way to Crystal River, Florida, and begin working as one of the service representatives at a car dealership. Her prayers for someone better, someone who also truly loved God, for love that overcomes all, and a man who would show her daughter the kind of love a father should would be answered when she met Frank.

Frank

*"Enter in through the narrow gate! Because the
gate is wide-and the way is broad- that leads to
destruction, and there are many who enter in
through it. Because the gate is narrow and the*

way is hard pressed which leads to life, and there are few who find it" (Matt. 7:13–14).

Just like with Rachel, the first time I saw Frank was when he was worshipping at the altar of our church. He, too, was being moved by the music, and the immense work God had done in his life was apparent by his expressions. While he was the second person I asked to interview, he was actually the ninth person I interviewed, due to scheduling conflicts. I was able to get to know Frank some during that time and realized that he is a mighty warrior of God. Frank has lived a version of hell on earth and escaped by the grace of God. He has used that freedom to bring people to God.

Frank grew up in Miami, Florida. He has a diverse cultural background of Italian, Cuban, and Irish. As he described it, he has an American side to his family and a Spanish side to his family. Frank and his parents lived in Hallandale, where the American side of his family lived, while the Spanish side lived in Hialeah. The neighborhoods Frank grew up in were not what you would consider good neighborhoods. In fact, they were downright bad areas.

Frank's parents were childhood sweethearts, but when Frank's mother became pregnant with Frank, his father was not ready to be a husband or father. Frank's maternal grandmother pushed the subject, and his parents married. However, being forced to become a father and husband did not have a positive impact on the relationship. Frank considers himself to have no father figure growing up. His dad only took him to the park once. Frank remembers that he would hide behind the couch from ten to eleven at night when his dad was home, just so he could be in his father's presence. When Frank was seven, his parents divorced. Despite the divorce, Frank's mother made sure he still had a relationship with his paternal grandparents. He would spend weekends at their house, and they played an active role in his life.

Divorce would pose a challenge for Frank and his mother with his mother's family though. His family was about 90 percent Jehovah's Witnesses, and divorce was highly looked down upon. When his mother divorced his father, they were kicked out of the church.

With no father figure and little guidance Frank began getting introduced to violence, drugs, and gangs at a very young age. When Frank was thirteen, he was introduced to gang life, and by fifteen, he was 100 percent involved. There were two gangs in his neighborhood: the older teens/adults and the younger teenagers. Frank was in the younger teen gang. They predominantly smoked and drank together. The older gang had an established history in gang activities. As a young boy in Frank's neighborhood, you basically started out in the younger gang and then moved up into the older gang.

> *"Do not be led astray, 'Evil company corrupts good habits'" (1 Cor. 15:33).*

About a year after Frank joined the younger gang, a rival gang moved into the neighborhood not far from where Frank lived. The rival gang terrorized the neighborhood. The neighborhood wasn't going to stand for it though. The entire neighborhood, including the two gangs of younger and older boys, united against the rival gang. What started out as defense grew out of control. There were many gun shots fired during the fight. This was Frank's first time witnessing gun fire and a higher level of gang violence.

The rival gang eventually left. The two local gangs remained joined in their illegal efforts due to the comradery created by fighting the rival gang. So, as a thirteen-year-old boy, Frank had to grow up fast and adjust to gang life including what it was like to be in a gang and go to school.

Frank enjoyed the "benefits" that being in a gang gave him during high school. Being in the gang garnered fear and a reputation that surpassed any single member. He only wore the colors that represented his gang and wore a "flag" (handkerchief) in his back pocket at all times. When kids were being bullied or beat up, they would come to Frank and ask him to handle the bully.

There was a "religion" to the gang. They had rules they needed to know, information that had to be memorized, and it was all contained within their "bible." As the years passed, the gang grew in size and power. They expanded from Broward–Dade to South Beach. Everyone knew the dope boy who sold weed, coke, or pills. They were the minor players, but as the gang grew, Frank began to meet major drug dealers. It was intriguing for him. He could make a lot of money or be taken out of the equation in seconds. The gang had a plan for Frank though as he had proved his worth as the "smart one." He would run logistics for the gang.

Frank ran a thirty-plus-member crew, with fifteen of them involved in the drug scene. He didn't think about the consequences because he didn't know anything different than the life he was living. He would spend hundreds of dollars on clothes and cars. People feared him. He could do whatever he wanted whenever he wanted. He felt powerful, except with cops. "The only gang we feared were the cops."

Even when it appeared that Frank was going deeper and deeper into the darkness, he still had a sense of morals. He would never allow the people below him to rob homes, old people, or to steal women's purses. He would tell his subordinates that there are just some people you do not steal from.

In this darkness, God still had a hand in Frank's life. At one point, Frank stared down a barrel of a gun, hearing the drop of the hammer, but no bullet was expelled due to a misfire. When asked how that felt, Frank explained that to be in a gang you have to feel dead on the inside. Fear had no place in gang life. It's what got you killed. So when the bullet didn't come out he was more surprised it didn't go off than he was fearful for his life. Frank also was in small and large brawls over the years. He got beat up and stabbed several times but was never seriously wounded. During drive-bys, shots were fired at him that by all accounts should have hit him, but they always missed. He had many friends who were shot and killed including his best friend. God was saving his life. He just didn't know why yet.

> "Deliver those taken to death, and hold back those stumbling to the kill" (Prov. 24:11).

During all this, Frank's mom was at a loss. She didn't know how to save her son. At seventeen, Frank beat up another kid in front of the kid's house. The kid's dad was a Vietnam Vet and did not take kindly to Frank's actions. Frank's mom decided it would be best for him to get out of Miami. She sent him to Texas to live with his dad. Frank's dad had opened a chicken restaurant in Texas, so she knew Frank would have a job while he was living in Texas.

When Frank was nineteen years old, he felt Jesus for the first time. He was in Fort Worth, Texas. He and a friend (from Miami) went to a mall, where an evangelist was speaking. The evangelist happened to be a former rival gang member. While the evangelist had been in the rival gang, he had killed one of Frank's friends. Frank went to the mall with every intention of killing the former gang member turned evangelist. Frank began speaking to the guy at the mall. They guy had no idea who Frank was. He kept talking to Frank about the Bible and God. Frank waited for an opportune time to kill him, but it never happened. Frank didn't expect to feel anything, but what the guy was saying resonated with him. Frank doesn't remember what he said specifically, but whatever the guy said had Frank attending church for the first time in a long time.

Frank and his friend (from Miami) went to the church they were invited to. The service reached Frank on a level he was not expecting, and he said the Prayer of Salvation. When saying the prayer, he felt a bubbling in his stomach. Frank felt like he was getting ready to speak in tongues, but he stopped himself. Afterward, they talked with the guy from the mall, and the guy explained being celibate. That ended Frank's interest in what the guy had to say. Shortly after attending church, Frank moved back to Miami and was re-immersed in the gang. But his time in church and with the evangelist from the mall was not lost on him. Frank's mind began to shift some.

While Frank was thoroughly entrenched in the gang including having the drug and alcohol addictions that went along with it, God was getting ready to open Frank's eyes in a way he would have never expected. Frank and some other members from the gang were doing reconnaissance on an individual that had done wrong by the gang. This person was a member of a rival gang. While Frank's gang had always used fists or knives, this rival gang started using guns. The individual he was watching had shot one of their gang members. Their orders were to kill said person when they came home, but that person never came home that night. Shortly thereafter, Frank found out that the person he was supposed to kill was a family member he didn't know from the Spanish side of his family. Frank's world became very small very quickly. He was mortified that he could have potentially hurt his family. Frank knew he had to find a way to get out of the gang.

Typically getting out of a gang is incredibly difficult, if not almost impossible. However, Frank knew exactly who to ask and what story to use in order to get out without any repercussions. In the gang Frank was in, they did have the rule that you could leave the gang if you wanted to pursue higher education. It was still difficult to get approved, but this is where Frank knowing who to talk to came in handy. It also helped that Frank was known as the "smart one." Frank told the leaders within the gang that he wanted to pursue an education in technology. They believed him and allowed him to step away from the gang. At twenty-one, eight years after he started gang life, Frank left, and never looked back.

When Frank left Miami, he left his pill addiction behind, but it would take years for him to overcome the addiction to alcohol, weed, and cocaine. Frank would spend the next few years moving from place to place across the country. His first move was to Phoenix, Arizona, for a couple years working at his dad's car dealership. Frank would then live in Las Vegas for a couple months. Eventually he would come back to Hialeah, Florida, for five years to take care of his grandmother whose health was deteriorating. Frank then decided to move to Ocala, Florida. He needed different surroundings in order to make the change in his life he knew he needed. He also needed to be closer to his mom as she was diagnosed with stage four cirrhosis.

God began to work on Frank in many different ways once he left Miami. Frank's first job in Ocala was at a car dealership. The dealership was owned by Christians. They would pray over each employee's paycheck prior to giving it to them. This introduced Frank to continual prayer. Something he had not witnessed before.

God was also working on Frank's ability to set aside his needs in order to help others. While in Ocala, Frank came to terms with the fact he had been a selfish child. His life became less about him and more about his mom. He wanted to make sure he did right by her as a way to make up for his teen years. It felt good to give so much to someone else. Taking care of his mom became a positive emotional experience that allowed him to begin to heal from some of his actions in his past.

Frank and his mom eventually moved from Ocala to Crystal River. His move to Crystal River would prove to be the place where God got a hold of him. Frank got another job at a car dealership. Much like at his first dealership job he encountered Christians. His manager would play gospel music. The first time Frank heard "I Can Only Imagine," it brought him to tears.

Frank was also beginning to be shown who he knew that was Pentecostal. Frank had a customer at the dealership who asked if she could pray for him. Frank cried immensely during her prayer. As they talked, they realized they both knew a family that Frank had lived near as a child. Frank was reconnected with the parents of a friend he grew up with. He thought they were regular bikers due to that being the lifestyle he saw and was scared of them as a child. As an adult, he realized they were major Pentecostal prayer warriors. When Frank reconnected with them, they introduced him to the Torah, and keeping the Sabbath on Saturdays.

Frank was also reconnected with another family that had lived on the block behind him in his youth. The parents had become Pentecostal evangelists that had been called to North Carolina. When the time would come for Frank to completely transform his life in Christ, he would drive to North Carolina to have them pray over him.

God was placing people in Frank's life that were guiding him in his faith. They were everyday people that God had changed and shaped their lives. God wasn't done guiding and placing people in Frank's life either. He was getting ready to introduce Frank to a woman who had overcome many battles and would forever change his life.

Rachel and Frank

"Beloved ones, let us love one another, because love is of Elohim, and everyone who loves has been born of Elohim, and knows Elohim" (1 John 4:7).

Both Frank and Rachel were brought to Crystal River, Florida, to be closer to their mothers. Frank had worked at the dealership longer than Rachel though. Because they worked together frequently, they began to start a friendship, but neither was looking for a relationship. Through the friendship Frank was able to learn about her faith, and Rachel learned about his mother's ailing health.

Frank had to leave work early one day, because his mother, who had been in the hospital for many days, was dying. As Frank was walking out of the hospital, God told him to call Rachel. Frank balked at the idea because he knew it was not the right time, but then God made it clear that he was supposed to. "When you have been alone your whole life, you know when someone else is there." Frank called Rachel.

Rachel was surprised Frank was calling her because she knew what he was going through. She picked up her phone, and Frank said, "Either I'm an idiot, or you like me too. Do you want to be with me? Because I want to be with you." Rachel was shocked by his statement, and just like Frank she hesitated because she was concerned about the timing of his call. However, she also felt the pull from God to say yes despite her concerns over him not being a Christian.

Rachel and Frank began dating. Rachel who wholeheartedly believed in the power of prayer for healing began going to the hospital every day to pray over Frank's mom. Frank's mom had already had her stomach tapped to remove water from her stomach. That procedure had the reputation of once it was done, it had to be done more regularly. It extended the life of the patient some, but ultimately was a death sentence. Rachel and Frank refused to believe that, despite her stomach being tapped three times. Rachel continued to pray every day, and against all laws of the natural Frank's mom began to heal. Upon her dismissal from the hospital the doctors still could not explain how she had lived. Frank and Rachel knew though. They knew that God had heard Rachel's prayers of healing and that they had been answered.

One week after they started dating, Rachel and her daughter moved in with Frank. Rachel already knew she wanted to marry him, but Frank still needed some time. About a month and a half after they started dating, Rachel took Frank to church with her. During the worship portion of service Frank saw Rachel's family go to the altar to worship, but she stayed back with him. He asked her afterward if she normally went up too. She said she did, but she didn't want him to feel uncomfortable. He told her to never let him hold her back from worshipping. The next week they went to church together again. She went up to the altar to worship. He stayed in his seat. On the third Sunday, Frank went to the altar to worship with her. On the fourth Sunday, Frank made the decision to get baptized, and on the fifth Sunday the Holy Spirit took a hold of him supernaturally. He has been on fire for God since then.

During this time of witnessing Frank's transformation, Rachel also began to be transformed. While she always had strong faith, she still felt like something was missing. However, witnessing Frank's transformation began to turn her heart even further toward God. It reignited her. Her path with God was a gradual growth whereas Frank was a stark transformation. Rachel had never seen that before, and she was filled with awe and appreciation. She realized that God was giving her everything she had ever prayed for in a man in Frank. She never had to try to coerce Frank into church, like exes from her past. God was moving within

Frank without her trying to make him have that connection. The Sunday Frank was baptized, Rachel rededicated herself.

Frank and Rachel became engaged shortly after their baptism and were married a month later. October 2020 was their one-year anniversary, and they have continued to see God's provision in their lives.

Shortly after their marriage Frank began to become conflicted over what he was dedicating his time to. He wanted to go to church on Sunday mornings and Wednesday nights, but his job required him to work during those times. Frank realized he wasn't doing anything for God. So he left his job where he was making $8000 a month and took a 50 percent pay cut to work for another dealership. He was now able to go to church and volunteer at the church.

Three months later, Frank went to get his haircut. His boss from the former dealership was there. He asked Frank, "What do we have to do to get you back?" Frank told him he needed Sundays off and had to leave work by five every Wednesday. The general manager of the dealership agreed so Frank returned. When Frank returned, he saw his income increase monthly from $4000 to $8000 to $10,000. Eventually, he was earning $20,000 in commission from his job, and each month he has tithed accordingly. Frank put God first, and God showed up in a big way for him.

God also gave Frank the opportunity to minister to those at his job. Since he has returned to the dealership, he has delivered seven of his coworkers to Jesus. The general manager of the dealership also allows Frank to pray for others, pray over the dealership, and pray over new employees.

> *"And let the pleasantness of Yahweh our Elohim be upon us, and confirm the work of our hands for us; O confirm the work of our hands!" (Ps. 90:17).*

God has also worked with Frank and Rachel to help her overcome her past. When Frank and Rachel were married, God placed it on Frank's heart that they were going to be attacked by Rachel's past, and gave Frank a patience he had never had before. When Rachel's past flared up Frank realized that he couldn't fully help if he was always reacting. He needed to be able to act first. He needed to have the strength to fight the demons from her past.

Frank began to pray to God, saying, "I need one second to be able to act vs react to the devil's attack." God gave him that. Frank then began to pray, "I need two seconds." God gave Frank that. Frank continued to pray for additional time, and each time his prayer was answered.

Rachel knew there were times that she was testing Frank. She had lived a life filled with violent men, and she didn't want to go through that again. However, seeing Frank's patience with her began to soften her heart. She saw Frank treating her daughter like his own, spending time with her and buying her things. Rachel saw that God had given her a man who loved and accepted her regardless of her past, and who gave her daughter the fatherly love she had never had. Rachel felt like God was showing her how much He loved her through Frank.

> *"And above all have fervent love for one another,*
> *because love covers a great number of sins"*
> *(1 Pet. 4:8).*

Both Frank and Rachel grew up predominantly without a father, and through their acceptance of God have realized that all those years without an earthly Father that they had and still have a father in heaven: God. Rachel realized that God never hurt her. She understands that it was the devil pulling her in the directions that led to violence and pain. It was God who pulled her out of her darkest moments. Rachel does not regret what she went through or what she has done. She believes that God was showing her that He had what she needed, but she just needed to listen. God continually reminded her that He loved her and showed her that she was worthy. Frank understood that all those times he stared down the barrel of a gun, was shot at in drive-bys but the bullets missed, or walked in and out of crack houses, that God was watching over him and protecting him in a way an earthly father never could. God had His hand in Frank's life and was guiding him.

> "Father of the fatherless...is Elohim in His set-apart dwelling" (Ps. 68:5).

Both Frank and Rachel have a passion for saving souls, and they see a future in evangelism. They want to be able to walk into dark places and be the light. They want to pray over people and help them to feel the restorative love of God. Neither of them felt worthy of being healed until God took a hold of them and showed them that with Jesus living within them, He makes them worthy. They want to share that love and worth with everyone.

God guided each of them in a manner that resonated with them. With Rachel, He continually calmly guided her. He showed her love, compassion, forgiveness and proved to her that she was worthy. With Frank, he staved off the bullets that could have ended Frank's life. God didn't force himself on Frank. When Frank was willing to open up and listen, He began to guide Frank toward a relationship with Him.

Frank and Rachel have both been through undeniably drastic and demonic moments in their lives. Yet through it all God had a plan for them. He had a plan to save each of them individually, and to bring them together to help save each other. God answered their prayers whether spoken or prayed in silence for a partner who would love them for what they have been through, what they have overcome, and who they are now in Christ. God has moved mightily in their lives and will continue to move them to new heights.

Chapter Four
A Lifetime Journey

E verybody's walk with God is different. There is no prescribed timeline as to when each of us will accept God into our lives or to gain a personal relationship with the one who created us. There is even a possibility that those two things do not happen at the same time.

My oldest daughter has had a love for God ingrained into her since she was very young. At three years old, she was asking me questions about God that I, at twenty-seven years old, had never asked. She wanted to go to Bible Study on Wednesday nights starting at four years old even when we as a family had never been to church. When she was six, she (and her four-year-old sister) voluntarily went to the altar to say the Prayer of Salvation and give their lives to God. They also both chose on their own to get baptized seven months after saying the Prayer of Salvation. Loving God and wanting to learn about him is one of her strongest desires in life. Whereas I knew about God and said the Prayer of Salvation while I was in Fellowship of Christian Athletes at twelve years old, but I never really accepted God into my life until I was twenty-five years old.

I was coming home really late one night from a work event in Orlando, and I cried almost the whole way home. I was crying about the job, my marriage falling apart, and the sheer weight of my life. It was over an hour drive, so I had plenty of time to think. By the time I pulled into the driveway I was in full hysterics. I didn't even open the gate before I flung open my car door and fell to my knees in the sandy driveway crying. I leaned back and looked up at the beautiful, starry country sky, and cried out, "God I can't do this by myself anymore! I need your help!"

I crumpled with my face just inches from the ground, and I felt a gentle breeze. Even though the car radio was still playing, and my door ajar alarm was dinging, it all faded. I felt the breeze and...peace. It was at that moment I no longer felt alone. It was also at that moment my life changed.

I believe we are all born with the innate desire to follow Him, to love Him and to feel his love in our lives. However, He understands that each person is uniquely and wonderfully made, and that those qualities do influence our walk with Him. He also knows that there are trials we face that may bring us to question his very existence. God is patient and does not mind that growing in our faith takes time. In fact, He expects our faith to continue growing over the course of our lifetime.

Jennifer

> *"He is saying of Yahweh, 'My refuge and my strong-hold, my Elohim, in whom I trust!'" (Ps. 91:2).*

College—also known as four years when I very poorly balanced my life. I would like to say that schoolwork was most important, but in reality, my social life reigned supreme. It was during this time of staying up until the wee hours of the morning partying with friends that I met Jennifer. She was a couple years older than me so the time we had together in college was brief, but she struck me as the kind of person who was much better at balancing her life than I. We ended up hanging out with the same group of people regularly, so we struck up an acquaintanceship.

After she graduated college, we remained connected through social media. Over the years, I would go on her social media page occasionally to see how she was doing, like or comment on a post, and she would do the same on my page.

When I started writing this book, Jennifer was placed on my heart as someone I needed to talk to. I knew it had been a really long time since we had seen each other, and we had never gotten to the point of where we would share life stories/struggles back in college. I put aside my concerns that she would think I was crazy. If God was placing her on my heart, I needed to reach out.

Jennifer grew up in a very Christian home. Her parents lived out their faith setting the example for their children. They sheltered Jennifer and her siblings from many of the hardships of the world. She took to heart what her parents taught her, but at the same time she was headstrong. Jennifer always considered herself a believer, but she was not always an achiever. She knew what the rules were, but she liked to test the boundaries.

When Jennifer was twenty, she met her first husband. They became physically involved very quickly and had more of a lustful relationship than a relationship filled with love. They married very quickly after meeting which Jennifer didn't think of as odd because her parents were married three months after they started dating. Unlike her parent's marriage, which would last until the parting of death, she realized very early on that her husband was not exemplar in the husband category. He lied frequently about what he was doing, and within six weeks of being married, he had cheated on Jennifer. Jennifer was not thrilled that he cheated, but she did not see it as a deal breaker. She believed that you must work at a marriage. When she said, "for better or for worse," she was not going to leave the minute the "for worse" appeared. She wanted to do her part to make things better. She realized though that his attitude about his actions was going to be the biggest hurdle. His philosophy was "you're the wife—deal with it." He had no intention of changing his cheating ways. She was devastated. He turned his cheating into her problem and not something he was concerned about. Jennifer's first marriage had officially ended.

After her first marriage, Jennifer was not honest with herself. She did not take time to let herself heal from the relationship. She didn't want to look bad or that she needed help. She adopted the philosophy of "shake it off and move on." However, this mentality would prove to lead her down a path of not only dishonesty with herself, but also with others.

Jennifer was in one relationship after another. None of them were right for her, and she began to inherit some of the negative traits from multiple failed relationships. Jennifer became unfaithful and promiscuous. The very traits that ended her marriage she now was involved in as well.

At twenty-two years old, Jennifer found out she was pregnant. She didn't hesitate in her decision. She made an appointment to get an abortion. Six weeks after her first abortion Jennifer found out she was pregnant again. She knew what she had done with the first abortion was not a good choice, and if she aborted this second baby it was not a good choice either. She felt like she had to do it. She was dating multiple guys and was not sure who the dad was. Technically, she was only supposed to be dating one guy too so she could have been caught cheating as well. Jennifer chose to have a second abortion.

When asked why she did not go to her parents, she responded that she felt ashamed and embarrassed. She did not think much about either abortion at the time, but when she did, she had regrets. At the time, she felt like it was her only option. Looking back now though she realizes that her mom would have made her feelings known but would have been there for her. She also knows that she would have had a candid conversation with her dad, but he too would have been supportive.

In 2008 at twenty-seven years old, Jennifer found herself jobless, so she had to move back in with her parents. Her personal life had already begun to calm down prior to moving home with her parents so this was a good transition. While living with her parents, she began going back to church. Yet every time she picked up the Bible it felt like fire. She didn't stop though. She knew she had to get back into the word.

In a Bible study group, she read the book *Surrendering the Secret*, by Pat Layton, and she began to find peace with her past. *Surrendering the Secret* is a Bible study book that "allows women to release this burden (shame and failure) and find freedom through 'redemptive community' while experiencing hope and joy, as shame and failure are replaced with beauty." Prior to the Bible study group, Jennifer felt like a horrible person for having multiple abortions. She considered herself a murderer. She was mad with herself because people would always comment how good she was with kids or that she would be a great mom when she had kids knowing in the back of her mind the two lives she had taken.

The Bible study group allowed Jennifer to fully acknowledge the choice she made, and to open up about her choice. It allowed her to be honest with herself, and to think about what her life would have been like if she had her children. It allowed her to acknowledge the regret she felt from having the abortions, but to also open up to God's redemptive grace. While she was in Bible study one night, she heard God call her name. It was the only time she had ever heard His voice. In that moment she realized she wasn't condemned. "He wouldn't call me if I was condemned."

Abortion is a topic that garners very intense feelings among many people. While I do not disagree with life being precious at any stage, and that abortions go against the Bible, when I hear Christians being so cold and stony in their expression toward women who have abortions it breaks my heart. I have lost count the amount of times I have heard visceral anger from a Christian for a person who commits abortion. No I do not advocate for abortion. I advocate kindness and actually following the tenants of the Bible.

> *"Do not judge, lest you be judged. For with what judgement you judge, you shall be judged. And with the same measure you use, it shall be measured to you" (Matt. 7:1–2).*

I believe (or at least would like to believe) that the vast majority of women who have an abortion do not take joy in it. I believe, from the conversations I have had with women who have had an abortion, they do it out of desperation, shame, guilt, and fear. Many of these women have felt like they had nowhere or no one to turn to for help. Many of them know what they are doing is wrong, and they do live with the shame and guilt for many years if not the rest of their life. Often, they hate themselves for their decision.

Now compound that guilt and shame they already feel with a Christian, someone who is supposed to show love and compassion as Jesus did, spewing hate or anger toward them. I'm not going to argue whether they were wrong or not in their choice for an abortion because I cannot change the past or their choice. I am going to ask you to take a good hard look at yourself. I want you to think about how you can be a positive example of Christianity when it comes to a difficult and polarizing topic.

When it comes to abortion, how can you help a woman (your friend, your sister, your daughter) know they are not alone? Are you going to recognize that there is a bigger problem that so many women feel like they don't have any other choice? How are you going react if you hear someone you know made the decision to have an abortion? Are you going to condemn them and write them off as sinners unworthy of God's redemption? Or are you going to ask them about their feelings and help show them the love God has shown you? Are you going to show them a way that brings them to light or are you going to compound their self-loathing? Are you going to put aside your own strong feelings and realize this person may be broken and hurting? Are you willing to recognize that God is willing to forgive *everyone*, not just who you find it convenient to forgive? Yes, you have every right to believe what you believe, and yes, it is backed by the Bible. But love, compassion, and forgiveness are also backed by the Bible.

> *"And be kind towards one another, tenderhearted, forgiving one another, as Elohim also forgave you in Messiah" (Eph. 4:32).*

Jennifer continued attending church frequently and was actively involved in Bible Study. She began picking up her Bible reading it and applying what she learned to her life. She wanted to live in a way that showed her faith.

> *"If we live in the Spirit, let us also walk in the Spirit" (Gal. 5:25).*

On New Year's Eve, 2014, Jennifer had the conversation of a lifetime with the man who would win her heart. She had always struggled fitting in never feeling comfortable in her own life.

This wasn't the case with Greg. When she talked to Greg, everything felt right, but there was a part of her past that she needed to let go.

Jennifer had a twelve-year on/off relationship with Julian, who was an atheist. During her time with Julian, she felt spiritually stagnant. Every time she walked into their apartment she would feel emotionally attacked. She believes him seeking out other entities hindered her ability to gain the kind of relationship she wanted with God. This on/off relationship was not good for her emotionally or spiritually, and she realized there was better out there. She needed to stop trying to be with someone who wasn't right for her.

Jennifer traded stagnancy for growth, in her relationships with both God and Greg. Greg became her husband and since meeting they have both been in a constant state of spiritual growth. They both love God, and Greg put a big focus on them serving God together. Tithing became automatically budgeted, and they also began to give to others. They began praying together regularly.

Jennifer and Greg both have strong personalities, but in different ways so it helps balance each other out. While Jennifer can't imagine not being married to Greg, getting married at thirty-four years old proved a bit challenging for her. She spent much of her adult life taking care of herself and following her own lead. Admittedly, letting her husband take the lead hasn't been easy.

Jennifer struggled immensely with his decision to quit his job and build his own business, even though it did not come as a surprise. Six months into them dating he told her he would start his own business one day. Jennifer just wasn't quite expecting "one day" to be the day it was. It was an income decrease that she was not quite willing to get used to, so she decided to get a second job. Yet even in her stubbornness to take care of it herself, she saw God come through for them time and time again.

When they were down to their last dollar, and not enough money for rent, Greg would get side hustles to make up the difference, she would get a call from the bank about accounts she had forgotten she had, or her job would need her to work overtime during a time when overtime was not expected. God always made sure they have been provided for.

Jennifer has also faced loss with Greg. Within the same year Jennifer and Greg both lost their mothers. Jennifer's mother was diagnosed with cancer. Jennifer would regularly stay with her in the hospital. Greg would bring her dinner. He would support her in any way possible. Sadly, Jennifer's mother would pass just ten months after her diagnosis. This was a very difficult time for Jennifer.

Jennifer felt that she had strength to get through the loss of her mother, but she prayed for her family during their time of mourning. Jennifer prayed for her brother to have strength during that time as he had lived the farthest away and was facing regret for not coming home as much as he could have. She prayed for her father to follow her mother's wishes that he remarry. Jennifer also prayed for her sister, who was very close to their mother and was having difficulty with the loss. However, like with her first marriage, Jennifer was not being honest with herself. She mentally locked up her grief. She recognized it hurt losing her mother but kept telling herself she was okay.

Eventually, Jennifer did realize that she was not okay. She knew that in order to get over the grief she had bottled up for years that she needed to talk about it. She went to therapy for four or five months and finally allowed herself to admit how she felt. As this trial began to be overcome, Jennifer started facing another trial.

The trial Jennifer is currently facing is infertility. When she first realized the hurdles that her and Greg were facing, she wondered if she was being punished for her actions more than a decade ago. That feeling was short-lived though. "God is not like that. Vindictive is a quality of mine, not His." She knew she had repented for what she had done ten years prior and had asked God for forgiveness.

> *"He who hides his transgressions does not prosper,*
> *but he who confesses and forsakes them finds*
> *compassion" (Prov. 28:13).*

She feels most vulnerable on Mother's Day and has allowed herself to openly cry with Greg. However, infertility has not tested her faith. She knows that God has His best for her, and that becoming pregnant will happen when it is supposed to. She has taken this time of difficulty to ask God what He wants her to do for His Kingdom and what lessons need to be learned.

While Jennifer absolutely has a relationship with God and is an avid prayer warrior for others, she has rarely prayed for herself. When I noticed the common theme of praying for others but not herself, I asked her why she has rarely gone to God over her own life. She responded that maybe subconsciously if she prays to Him for her needs then she is relying on Him, and she has always relied on herself to get through things. Jennifer has not yet gotten to the point of relinquishing control of her life over to God.

Relinquishing control and giving everything (your hopes, dreams, troubles) over to God is hard. I believe people as a whole want to be in control of our lives. Having control gives us a false sense of security. Yet if there is one thing I have learned in the last seven years of my life since giving God control, is when I renege and try to control things, that is when it all gets messed up. That is when I feel like I am beating my head against a brick wall. No forward movement can be done. It is when I renege that

I find myself swallowing my pride and humbling myself before God handing Him back the reins to my life.

Now, is Jennifer a bad Christian for not yet relinquishing control of her life and praying for herself? Absolutely not! She, like every other person in this book and on this planet, is a work in progress. This just so happens to be the place where she is in her walk. Does God want her to get to the point of giving Him control over her life? Absolutely! Because He has big plans for her that can only be attained through Him. Will God rush or force her to get to that point? Absolutely not! He will work on her over and over if needed to help her reach her full potential and purpose. God will be patient with her just as He is patient with you and me.

Jennifer has walked a path that many may have strong opinions about. The only truly important opinion is God's, and as we can see His love and redemption are all over her life. She has made the choice to change her life living it as an example of Him for which He recognizes. She continues to grow in her faith and be of service to Him. Her old life is gone, and the new life has God at the heart of it.

> *"Yahweh is not slow in regard to the promise, as some count slowness, but is patient toward us, not wishing that any should perish but that all should come to repentance" (2 Pet. 3:9).*

Chapter Five
Even Christians Face Trials

Think about the most challenging moment in your life. Was it painful? Were you afraid? Did you feel alone, rejected, or humiliated? Did you curse God and ask him why? Or was God not even in your thought process?

Now I want you to find the good that came from it. Did you acquire new strength? Did you break the chains of bondage? Did you meet someone or go somewhere that led you to a new beginning? Was someone else's life saved due to your misfortune? Did you find God reaching out to you to help you?

Everybody—let me repeat that—*everybody*—is going to face trials in their lives. Some are in part due to our bad choices. Some trials are going to happen due to the actions that others do to you. Then there are others in which the devil is at work, and that is when we need to say, "Get thee behind me, Satan." No matter how "Christian" you are, you are going to face trials. Yet, it is our perspective that can change our lives and our relationship with God.

> *"My brothers, count it all joy when you fall into various trials, knowing that the proving of your belief works endurance. And let endurance have a*

perfect work, so that you be perfect and complete, lacking in naught" (James 1:2–4).

When people are going through trials, *joyful* is probably not the first word that comes to their minds. However, you do often hear people say that they wouldn't be who they are today without their trials. They are thankful for what God helped them get through. They are thankful that they can use their trials to help others or that their trials led to a new path in life.

God does not exempt you from trials once you accept Him into your life because he knows that iron sharpens iron. He knows that the fires you walk through will allow Him to pour miracles into your life. God is working on you through those trials to help bring you to the place you are supposed to be and become the person He knows you are meant to be.

> *"O Yahweh, I know the way of man is not in himself, it is not for man who walks to direct his own steps" (Jer. 10:23).*

Stephanie

> *"I have strength to do all, through Messiah who empowers me" (Phil. 4:13).*

There are times when you hear pieces of someone's story that make you think, "Wow, they have come a long way." I had very few interactions with Stephanie prior to the Homeschool Mom's Christmas party, in December 2019, but when she stood up to share a devotional at the party, I was blown away by how raw and honest she was. To be truthful, I don't even remember the devotional. What I remember is a woman sharing the love of God in a room full of women, many of which she barely knew. I watched her as she began to cry, and my heart broke for her. I watched her struggle through the tears to say everything she wanted to share. Yet I was inspired. I was inspired but her willingness to share the bad in a way that highlighted God's mercy and love.

I talked with Stephanie briefly after the Christmas party, but we wouldn't connect again until God told me to write this book. I find it beautiful how God creates momentary interactions that leave an impact. Stephanie had no idea how much she touched my heart that night, and at the time, I had zero inkling that I was going to be writing a book the next year. But God knew. He knew it all, and when he told me to write, Stephanie was at the forefront of my mind.

For the majority of her youth Stephanie grew up in a non-believing, alcoholic home. Stephanie's dad would try not to drink at home, but he was angry all the time. Everyone would be walking on eggshells as they did not want to face his wrath. He would discipline out of anger beating them with a belt until they couldn't sit. These actions began to build resentment within Stephanie toward her dad. He would also be gone for days at a time including her tenth birthday. When he did come home, if Stephanie showed sadness over his actions, he called her a cry baby. Her mother tried to protect the kids, but unfortunately ended up in fights with her husband. Stephanie remembers her mom asking her dad why he was doing this to them. She also remembers her dad being drunk and high trying to set the shed on fire.

Despite her home life, Stephanie was allowed to attend church, and she loved the Lord as a child. At twelve, she was saved alongside her mother, but her true salvation moment would come years later. Her dad would also attend church. He went to AA, and tried to change, but it would only be for about ten months.

Like many other nights, Stephanie's dad did not come home on a Saturday evening. When Stephanie's mother was driving her and the children to church, they saw Stephanie's dad's car at the house of a woman they knew. Stephanie's mother pulled into the driveway and went up to the house. When the woman answered the door, she asked her, "Where is my husband?" Stephanie couldn't hear the words that were exchanged past that point, but she knew it wasn't good. After the conversation, Stephanie's mom kept their focus on God and still attended church. That would mark the end of the marriage between Stephanie's mom and dad.

> *"He who commits adultery with a woman lacks heart; He who does it destroys his own life"* (Prov. 6:32).

Not only did Stephanie face an abusive early childhood at home, but also at school. Stephanie had a strong personality, but due to extreme bullying she developed a very calm personality. School was rarely a safe place for Stephanie. She hoped that if she was quiet people wouldn't notice her. She felt like a sitting target.

At five years old, Stephanie attended a Christian school. While playing in a house in the classroom a little boy showed Stephanie his privates and said they were supposed to play with each other. This would be the first of many inappropriate encounters Stephanie would have, but the majority of her experiences would be with older female classmates.

Throughout elementary and middle school Stephanie would be bullied and molested many times by female classmates. One time, Stephanie decided she had had enough of the bullying and defended herself. Her years of anger came out, and she beat up a girl using a chair. Despite the anger over the bullying and molestation, Stephanie began to have a homosexual spirit at the age of fourteen. She began fantasizing about girls. She felt slightly convicted as a Christian, but since she was still new to Christianity, she didn't change her mind.

At fourteen years old, her mother remarried. Stephanie's stepfather had been best friends with her biological father for years. He was actually the husband of the woman who had been caught cheating with Stephanie's biological father. Prior to their marriage, Stephanie's mom did not like this man, but he was a smooth talker. He worked his way into Stephanie's mom's life and home.

The abuse Stephanie received from this "father figure" would alter her way of thinking for years. He was a verbal abuser. He would repeatedly call her names as well as speak anger and doubt over her and her life. He did this so much that she began to believe him. Her personality changed. She went from being a very calm person to a very angry person. She learned to cut people down in seconds with her words. She would use sarcasm to push people away. Her life became abusive, angry, and hostile. She watched as her stepdad would act horribly at home but would go to church on Sunday and act like a man of God. She got angry with God. If He is so great, then why was he putting her through this?

Stephanie dismissed her choice to live for God and chose to live for herself. By eighteen, she was smoking, drinking, going to underground clubs, getting intimate with other women, and couch hopping was a means to keep a roof over her head. Stephanie no longer cared about God. She let her anger toward God grow and would do what she could to contradict God. Why should she care about what she was doing? Her life was a mess. Even when we push God away, He is still willing and able to work miracles in our lives.

After a couple years of living for the here and now Stephanie decided to try to get her life together. She was tired of nothing changing and continually meeting messed up guys. She moved in with a friend and began working at a steady job.

Sometimes getting your life together is done in steps which was the case for Stephanie. While some things were becoming steadier like her job, she was still frequently out partying. When she and a friend were at work, they were discussing the guys that would be taking them to Ybor that night. Stephanie knew one of the guys, but the other, Tom, was a friend of his that she had never met. Stephanie's coworker said the guys were going to come into their work that day. When Stephanie saw Tom, she knew she was going to marry him. There was a catch, though.

Tom didn't like girls who partied. While he didn't mind having fun, dating someone who partied multiple times a week was not ideal. So, while she knew immediately, she was going to marry him, it took some time before Tom knew it too.

All of Stephanie's previous relationships had no restraints so she was used to the relationship becoming physical quickly. Tom immediately put boundaries in place. He did not want to get physical. He wanted to get to know her better. Stephanie was used to getting what she wanted right away, but she could appreciate Tom's use of boundaries. They talked a lot. He didn't smoke either, so many times they would sit outside and talk. He listened to her, which was new and refreshing for Stephanie. Tom was stable, calm, and consistent. He was many things that she had never known in her life. He also was going to college and working. Their acquaintanceship became a budding friendship, which eventually led to a relationship.

During their relationship, Stephanie lost her job due to continually coming in late. She knew she needed a job and fast, as that was something that was important to Tom. She had a guy friend who worked at a strip club and told her he could get her a job. Stephanie applied for the job and got it. She was very excited and thought Tom would be too.

She never could have guessed Tom's response to her getting a job as a stripper. While all her exes would have been thrilled, Tom was not happy at all. He told her he could not be with someone who would dishonor themselves like that. Stephanie was floored. She realized Tom was truly unlike any other man she had ever had in her life. He honored her and wanted the best for her. She declined the job as a stripper and looking back at it now realizes God used Tom to save her from a life worse than what she could have imagined.

Stephanie fully gave up her partying lifestyle for something a little simpler: life in the country with her boyfriend.

> "But those who wait on Yahweh renew their strength, they raise up the wing like eagles; they run and are not weary, they walk and do not faint" (Isa. 40:31).

Imagine getting up to answer the phone (back when we all used landlines and the phones were attached to the wall). So, you hear the phone ring. You get up. You walk to the phone. Somehow, in the process of walking to the phone you fall, and you break your leg. Now imagine yourself back at home after seeing the doctor. You live way out in the country. You only have three stations that come in on the TV. You don't have cable or internet, and cell phones were only a thing that the extremely wealthy had. Oh, yeah, and you can't move all that much because you have a broken leg. Sounds fun right?

Well this is the exact situation Stephanie found herself in at nineteen years old. She had three stations to watch and limited mobility. God took this time of limited mobility to work on

Stephanie. While she was doing much better with stability in her physical life (minus the broken leg), she was still unstable spiritually. Joyce Meyers Ministry was one of the only programs that came through on her three-channel TV. Stephanie began to feel extreme conviction over her past and choices she had made. She cried immensely over her past, and she opened her heart to God again feeling his redeeming spirit. She would spend the next four to five months feeding herself the Word of God. But God wasn't done with Stephanie yet. He sent an unlikely messenger to bring her back to the church.

About a month after she opened back up to God, a guy came to Stephanie's door asking to use her phone. (Again, this was before everyone had a cell phone. It was also during a time when letting a stranger into your house wasn't as unwise as it is now.) He was doing clean up at a construction site nearby, and he had a flat tire. He needed to call someone to come and help him. Stephanie felt at peace with his presence. It was a very benign encounter until he got off the phone and proceeded to ask her if she knew Jesus. That conversation led to an invitation from him for her and Tom to attend an event at the church he went to which just so happened to be the church that Stephanie grew up in. Before he left, he prayed for her. Stephanie felt like God had sent her an angel. She was open to his prayer and in awe of how God was working at that moment. She felt incredibly special for God to have this man cross her path.

Stephanie and Tom began to attend the church they had been invited to. It was weird at first going back to church, since she hadn't been in years. She was also a little concerned what Tom would think of the church. He was raised Baptist, and the church was Pentecostal. They both enjoyed the church though and felt at home. Just a few months later they were married on a Sunday before service was held.

There was one thing that was still really nagging at Stephanie during the first four years of their marriage. While she had ultimately chosen to spend her life with her husband, she was still having fantasies about women. She no longer wanted to feel those homosexual tendencies. "I couldn't take it anymore." She cried out to God to remove the homosexual spirit. When she called out, she felt like something was lifted off of her. Stephanie never looked nor thought about a woman in a sexual way ever again.

Stephanie and Tom have been together for twenty years now, and, as she so beautifully put it, God used him to rescue her. Between her biological father, stepfather, and the boyfriends she had prior to her husband, she admittedly had a skewed view of what a man should be like. This skewed view caused many occasions where she would try to push her husband away because she felt it was too good to be true. She believes, though, that when God brought her husband into her life it was God's way of saying "Let me show what a real man is like." Tom showed her love like she had never known. He provided for her, and even after twenty years, he has never spoken an ill word to her. She believes she has seen a lot of Jesus through him.

> "Yahweh appeared to me from afar, saying, "I have loved you with an everlasting love, therefore I shall draw you with loving-commitment" (Jer. 31:3).

Besides being partners in life, Stephanie and Tom both served together as youth pastors for seven years. During her time as a youth pastor, Stephanie still smoked three packs of cigarettes a day. She knew smoking was not biblically correct, but, as anyone who is or knows a smoker, quitting is very hard. Years later she found out that during this time a mother of a child she taught in the youth group approached the pastor about her smoking. This mother couldn't believe that the pastor would let Stephanie work for the church when he knew she smoked. The pastor simply responded that they should pray for God to help Stephanie. Shortly after that conversation happened, Stephanie found out she was pregnant with their first daughter. She immediately quit smoking and has not smoked since.

This interaction, I believe, shows two sides of what people see when they look at Christians. The doctrinal Christians (the mother) who pass judgment, and the compassionate Christians (the pastor) who choose to pray for God to help someone instead of demeaning them. I want you to take a moment to think about which kind of Christian you are or are working toward becoming. Which one do you think shows the love of Jesus Christ better? While I have no idea who this mother is, and she very well may have regretted what she said the moment the pastor said let's pray for Stephanie, we must be wise with our words. We can disagree with someone's personal choices, but we as Christians should not be condemning them. We should be praying for them, and if possible, extending a hand to help them. Imagine being a kid and your parents are constantly telling you how wrong you are. You wouldn't want to listen to them anymore. It's the same for Christians. If we are constantly telling people how many times they are going against the word of God, they won't want to listen. But if you are kind, helpful and show what the love of God can do in people's lives your light will be so bright everyone will want what you have.

> *"But maintaining the truth in love, we grow up in*
> *all respects into Him who is the head, Messiah"*
> *(Eph. 4:15).*

As Stephanie and Tom were starting a family of their own, she was faced with how to incorporate her father who was still an alcoholic into her children's lives. Their relationship had faltered over the years, because, as she grew out of her partying ways, he no longer had a reason to hang out with her. Alcohol had been their connection in her late teens and that connection was no longer there. Yet Stephanie still wanted her children to know their grandfather. She was also in her own way still seeking the approval he had yet to give her.

When her daughters were three and five years old, she let them go over to her dad's house for part of the day. When she came to pick them up, she found him drunk and the kids watching a horror movie he had on the TV. It was at this moment she knew she couldn't let her kids grow up in the same toxic environment she grew up in throughout her early childhood. This didn't mean she no longer loved her father. It meant that the toxicity had to stop. No matter how many times she tried to help him or offer an opportunity to change he wasn't willing to take it. She had to distance herself and her children from him. Stephanie was angry and hurt.

> *"Be wroth, but do not sin. Do not let the sun go down on your rage, nor give place to the devil. Let him who stole steal no more, but rather let him labour, working with his hands what is good, so that he has some-what to share with those in need" (Eph. 4:26–28).*

Anger is one of those emotions that is very one-sided. Rarely does the person you are angry with feel what you feel, especially if they don't feel they were in the wrong. They may know that you are angry, but they don't feel the ache in your heart, the knots in your stomach, the rollercoaster of emotions. They don't see your sleepless nights or tears falling down your cheeks as you come to grips with their actions. A constant feeling of anger toward a person hurts you more than it hurts the other person. God does not want you to bear feelings of anger or sadness forever. He wants you to be happy. Take your anger and sadness to him. Ask him to help you overcome these emotions and to find peace and joy once again.

> *"Come to me, all you who labour and are burdened, and I shall give you rest"* (Matt. 11:28).

For years Stephanie bore the burden of the anger and hurt she felt from her father, but in time God began to lighten her load. He allowed her to feel her dad's heart. While Stephanie's dad was more of the absentee drunk dad, his father would regularly physically abuse him. Stephanie began to understand that unfortunately her father had become a product of his childhood and had been unable to overcome the anger, pain, and emotional trauma his father had inflicted upon him. Her anger and sadness began to subside, and she began to forgive her father. Forgiveness opened her heart so that she wanted to reach out to him, but she was unsure how that interaction would turn out. God spoke to her and told her that when they spoke, her father would not apologize. God told her "You have to have acceptance from Me, because I am your Father." When Stephanie reached out to her biological father to reconcile, he did not apologize, like God had told her. However, she understood him better and his broken promises no longer hurt like they did before.

No one is perfect. We all have instances where we make rash decisions or speak before we think. Like many others, Stephanie recognizes that she is a work in progress. Her years of being sarcastic and lashing out still have an impact on her and her family. She admits there are times where she has lost her temper with her children and husband. There have been times where she has had to sit them down and apologize for her actions. Stephanie has also used these times to come to God. She uses these times to die to herself and let God take the reins.

> *"Every branch in Me that bears no fruit He takes away. And every branch that bears fruit He prunes, so that it bears more fruit" (John 15:2).*

Every time Stephanie dies to herself, she feels like she is losing herself, but gaining an identity in Christ. It is scary for her at times, but she surrenders again and again to God. This allows her to build a closer relationship with God and to open up more to Jesus within her.

One of Stephanie's biggest prayers throughout her life has been that her daughters remain pure and live a better life than she did. Stephanie attributes her promiscuous past to the molestation she faced at a young age, and that is something she wanted to protect her daughters from. Stephanie has seen God answering her prayer. When Stephanie's oldest daughter was eleven, they attended a wedding where the bride and groom's first kiss was at the altar. Stephanie's daughter was in awe of that and has held onto that moment for several years. Even at seventeen years old, Stephanie's oldest daughter still wants to save her first kiss for the wedding altar. Stephanie is also seeing her youngest daughter who is just entering her teen years starting to follow her sister's choice of saving her first kiss for the altar. Spring is incredibly thankful for what God is doing with her daughters as it is a stark contrast from her teen years. She is watching generational curses being broken in her family.

For the last five years Stephanie felt like she was in a personal spiritual dry season. She did not feel the connection with God like she had in the past, and it seemed as if her prayers (outside of her daughter's remaining pure) didn't make it past the ceiling. She felt physically fatigued every time she opened her Bible. When she read the Bible, the words made it to her head but not her heart. She struggled with even knowing if she was saved. How could this happen to a woman who for twenty years had such a strong faith in God?

Since Stephanie was fourteen years old, she has wanted to go on mission trips. She had a vision of herself in a country with little kids. That vision has never left her heart. A little over five years ago, she started planning a mission trip for her family. There were a couple of things that needed to be addressed prior to this family mission trip. The first was her husband. While Tom enjoys sharing and teaching the word of God, five years ago, he had no desire to travel across the world to share the word. The planning was also put to a halt when she began to care for her husband's grandfather. He was in the final years of his life, so Stephanie and Tom began to take care of him. Her focus shifted from mission work to taking care of family and completing her degree in theology.

Over the course of the five years she was helping take care of Tom's grandfather and completing her degree, God began planting the seed of mission work in her husband's heart. Tom began having ideas about the mission work he could be involved in and gained a passion for sharing the word of God with others around the world. Stephanie believes that the last five years God has tasked her with focusing on more earthly things so that He could work on her husband. This transformation within her husband has also allowed for more unity within their relationship. Now they have a family mission trip planned for Africa that every member of the family is excited about.

So often we wonder why we can't reach our goals when we feel like we are ready. Stephanie was ready to go on a mission trip. She was ready to share the word of God with children across the world, but she didn't want to do it alone. She wanted her family to be a part of it too. There are times where God will put a hold on what you want to do because the people who are meant to help you along the way are not ready yet. In this instance, it is apparent who was not ready yet: Stephanie's husband. But what do you do when you can't see or don't even know the person who is supposed to help you?

> *"Trust in Yahweh with all your heart, and lean not on your own understanding; Know Him in all your ways, and He makes all your paths straight"* (Prov. 3:5–6).

You must wait for God. If you try to kick and shove your way toward your goals, you will hit roadblock after roadblock. When was the last time you reached a goal 100 percent on your own? You received no input, encouragement, inspiration, training, tips or assistance from anyone. I would venture a guess that would be never. There is usually at least a friend, family member or coworker who you share your goal with, and they say, "You can do it!"

God will clear a path for you when the timing is right: when you have learned the lessons, gained the knowledge, but also when the people meant to help you have learned the lessons and gained the knowledge. He also knows your heart and listens to your prayers. God is a God of wonders. He can make the impossible possible. You must be patient enough to wait for the answer to your prayers. Don't try to shove your way past God's provision. Listen to Him and take heed.

Stephanie continues to grow as a wife, mother, and child of God. She continues to strive for a better relationship with each as well. She also continues to face trials. However, her life is filled with God's redemption, love, and healing. Her trials will be overcome as she continues to seek God. He has and always will be watching over her and guiding her. There is no trial she will ever face that He will not be alongside her.

Chapter Six

He Breaks your Chains

There is a song by Tasha Cobbs called "Break Every Chain," that I literally had on repeat for an entire work day. I must have sang/cried along to that song a dozen times over the course of the day. I paid attention to every word and it hit me so hard, but when I looked up the lyrics I realized that it repeated "There is power in the name of Jesus" twelve times and "To break every chain" thirty times! When I was singing along, I didn't realize that this song that was hitting every fiber of my being was literally repeating the same thing over and over. Why did this song that had very little variation from lyric to lyric hit me so hard?

Visualize a chain. What do you see? I think most of you see strong metal links fastened together. What do you use chains for? Again, I think most of you would have said one of these words: secure, fasten, tether, bind, restrain, shackle, confine, or imprison.

Think about your life. Can you use any of the words above to describe an aspect of your life? Do you feel bound by grief? Do you feel imprisoned in an abusive relationship? Do you feel shackled to a job you hate? Do you feel restrained because of addiction? Do you feel tethered to a diagnosis? Do you feel confined within a traumatic event? What has or is happening in your life right now that makes you feel chained?

Now, I want you to think about Jesus. Yes, Jesus died on the cross to bear our sins, but His name is also the name that makes demons flee. Even the devil knew what Jesus meant for us to the extent of offering Jesus all the kingdoms of the world. "And the devil, taking Him up on a high mountain, showed Him all the reigns of the world in a moment of time. And the devil said to Him, "All this authority I shall give You, and their esteem, for it has been delivered to me, and I give it to whomever I wish" (Luke 4:5–6).

The devil knew that if Jesus was to perform the ultimate sacrifice and die for our sins that he (the devil) was to lose the war. That Jesus's name would be so powerful that it would make those against Him flee, and that the utterance of His (Jesus's) name would have the power to change someone's life.

The devil wants to see you chained. In fact, he is all too happy to burden you with chain after chain until you are so burdened that the idea of looking up and calling out to Jesus is exhausting. But that is what we must do. We need to recognize our chains and call upon Jesus to break the chains. Break the chains of violence. Break the chains of grief. Break the chains of addiction. We must regain our freedom and peace in Christ Jesus. It was Jesus's death on the cross and resurrection that gave us redemption, a chance at forgiveness, an opportunity to do His (God's) works on Earth, and the ability to have everlasting life in Heaven.

We must not be so proud that we can't humble ourselves during trials and realize that we are not enough. We must learn to appreciate the moment God strips us of ourselves and open our hearts to God knowing that His plan is far better than ours. We are not meant to bear every burden alone. We are meant to have a Lord and Savior that walks beside us and carries our yoke. We are meant to cry out "Jesus!" when the devil is placing chain after chain upon us. We must also believe with everything inside of us that the name of Jesus has the power to break every chain.

So, to answer the question as to why the song hit me so hard is simple. Because I have seen the chains that have been placed upon my life broken when I have cried out to Jesus. I have slammed hard into rock bottom and been picked up. I have cried out for forgiveness, help and peace and received all of them.

"For the torah of the Spirit of the life in Messiah Yeshua has set me free from the torah of sin and of death" (Rom. 8:2).

Carolyn
> *"Loveliness is deceptive and prettiness is vain,*
> *a woman who fears Yahweh is to be praised"*
> *(Prov. 31:30).*

I received a message one day from a friend asking me to call her as soon as possible. From the urgency in the message, I called her immediately. After two rings she picked up. Before I could even ask what had happened, she began telling me about something incredible that had happened to her that morning.

"Sarah, I was walking with Carolyn, and we were talking about things completely unrelated to your book. Suddenly, God spoke to me and told me that I needed to tell her about your book. I know you aren't sharing with many people that you are writing this book yet, so I hope you aren't mad at me. Carolyn has an incredible story though of how God has worked in her life, and she is willing to share it with you."

Of course, I wasn't mad. In fact, it was at that moment that I silently thanked God. Two days prior to this call, I had prayed, "God I know that I do not know all the people who are supposed to be in this book. Please guide me to them or bring them to me."

God answered my prayer. The friend who called was one of maybe ten people that knew I was in the beginning stages of writing this book. She didn't know I had said this prayer, but God knew. He put all the pieces together.

Carolyn grew up in a Christian home. Her dad was an assistant minister at a Lutheran Church. She grew up going to Sunday School, and knew about Jesus's life. While she was taught to memorize scriptures, she was not taught about having a personal relationship with God. She also did not see much of the church within her home. Her parents were good people, but when it came to praying, the only prayer she ever saw inside the home was her dad praying before dinner. As a young girl and teenager, Carolyn believed that being Christian meant you were able to check all the boxes off by getting baptized, confirmed and attending Sunday school. She wasn't sure what it was to be Christian past checking the boxes.

Outside of the home, Carolyn was a big fish in a small pond. She came from a small town and was an all-star athlete in basketball, track, and volleyball. She was undefeated in hurdles her sophomore and junior year of high school. She was part of the popular crowd and enjoyed her place among them even allowing them to influence some of her choices. Carolyn had joined friends a couple times at parties and drank a couple times. However, she was not big into partying or drinking because sports were her priority. If she had been caught, she would have been suspended from sports, and that was not an option Carolyn was willing to take.

When Carolyn was sixteen, she was invited to a party at a guy's house that she went to school with. The party was in a large shed at the guy's house that they called the barn. It was a frequent party spot for kids at the high school. She realized when she pulled up it was more of a hangout than a party. There were five guys and another girl that she knew from school at the barn.

Carolyn figured that since there were so few people that they would just be hanging out.

It turned out that there was alcohol at the party. Since Carolyn had drank alcohol so infrequently, she was still learning how it affected her. She had a couple drinks at the party, and they affected her more than expected.

At one point during the party, she remembers two of the guys taking her upstairs to the loft. She didn't think anything of it at the time as the loft had a bed so she thought they were taking her up there so she could sleep for the rest of the night. Her surroundings were going in and out of focus as they entered the loft. They laid her down, and she began to drift to sleep, but one of the guys began to advance upon her. She was in shock. No one had asked her if she wanted sex, and she was petrified how to respond to their advances. She didn't know how to make it stop. This was a guy from her school. They knew each other. Why was he doing this? She didn't say no, but she didn't want it. She didn't participate at all. She hoped that if she didn't move, he would stop.

When he was done with her, he left so she thought it was over. She was still in shock, afraid to move, and was going in and out of consciousness. During a moment of coherence, she heard that the other guys had come in. She could hear them talking over her but couldn't make out what they were saying. It didn't matter what they said, though, because one by one all five guys raped her.

Carolyn doesn't remember many of the specifics, but at one point, one of the guys flipped her over onto her stomach. She just wished she could disappear into the bed. When the other girl from the party came up to check on what was going on, the guys blocked her from coming all the way up and sent her back downstairs. Carolyn remained in shock and disbelief the entire time. She couldn't believe these guys, who she thought were her friends, were doing this to her. When they had all had their turn one of the guys took her home.

The weekend following her rape was a blur. She tried to block the memories from the night out of her mind. Since she was from a small town, Carolyn chose to not tell anyone including her parents what happened that weekend. She wanted to avoid confrontation and just put it behind her. It was also a way for her to cope with what had happened to her. She already blamed herself and felt like sharing would make it worse.

Monday, two days after she had been raped by five guys from her school, Carolyn decided to still go to school, knowing that she would see her rapists walking the halls. Walking down the hallway of the school, she saw her friend who was the girlfriend of one of her rapists. Her friend looked furious. Carolyn was confused. She hadn't told anyone she had been raped, let alone who had raped her. Her friend started yelling at her, calling her a whore and slut. She started yelling at Carolyn for sleeping with the five guys that weekend one of which was her boyfriend. Apparently, this girl's boyfriend had gone back to his girlfriend's place and told her about what had happened. Instead of waiting to see if Carolyn would tell anyone, he chose to twist the story telling his girlfriend that Carolyn had slept with all of them that night of the party. When Carolyn was being yelled at in the middle of the hallway, she instantly wanted to die. She also couldn't understand how the girl was not mad at her boyfriend. All day long classmates called her names. No one, not even her closest friends, asked her what happened. What she was being accused of was completely out of character for Carolyn. So why was no one asking to hear her side? Carolyn didn't expect people to respond that way. She began to question herself. Was it really rape if she didn't verbally say no? Was she a whore?

There is a section of Colossians 3:12 that says "Therefore, as chosen ones of Elohim, set-apart and beloved, put on compassion, kindness, humbleness of mind, meekness and patience..." Imagine what Carolyn must have felt like to still be processing that level of horror and being bombarded with such despicable accusations. When you are presented with information whether it be about a friend, family member or a stranger, you must realize there are two sides to every story. Recognize this and take a moment to think before you react. Do not act out of anger, frustration, or hurt. Take time to gather your thoughts, think about it from the other person's perspective, and if needed calmly talk to the person in question. Can you imagine how different things may have been if even one of Carolyn's friends had asked for her side of the story? Be willing to be a compassionate friend or family member. Be willing to have a difficult conversation, but do it with patience and gentleness. Do not be defensive or judgmental. There may be times that we do not want to hear the truth, and that may have been the case with Carolyn's friends. Some may have realized that the story did not sound right and may have assumed the truth. However, they were not willing to have that hard conversation. That's when you have to put on the heart of humility. Put aside the importance of your comfort and realize that others may need to be comforted.

In response to the rape and accusations of being a whore, Carolyn threw herself into drugs and alcohol. It was easier for her to process that she was a slut than being raped. If she allowed herself to begin to acknowledge the rape, she would become angry and filled with rage.

Sex became meaningless, and one-night stands were a regular occurrence. She used the lack of emotion she felt toward sex as a way to take the power back that she had lost. If guys wanted sex, but it meant nothing to her, then she had better control over the situation.

Drugs and alcohol led to a decline in her athletic abilities. As a senior, Carolyn did not come in first place in the hurdles. She placed third. Shortly after that, Carolyn stopped participating in sports, and passed up many scholarships. She still graduated high school and went on to college, but the path she took was far different than the one expected.

Her drug and alcohol addiction followed her to college. Two years into college, Carolyn became suicidal. She remembered where her life was headed prior to being raped, and she saw where her life was now. She was miserable. For the first time in a while she prayed to God "If you do want me to exist, please save me."

While she had not been living with God in her life for four years, Carolyn believes that the foundation her parents set for her through regular church attendance in her younger years played a big role in how she handled her life choices at twenty.

"Train up a child in the way he should go, even when
he is old he turns not away from it" (Prov. 22:6).

While she never told her mom, what happened to her when she was sixteen, Carolyn's mom was a domestic violence counselor, and recognized that Carolyn was showing signs of being a rape victim: paralyzing anxiety, depression, getting heavily involved in drugs, and having an eating disorder. While Carolyn was still living at home, her mom had left pamphlets on her dresser about rape and drugs. Her mom did not judge or pry but tried to help her daughter in a way she thought Carolyn may be open to. So when Carolyn called at twenty years old asking to be taken to rehab, her mom didn't hesitate to take her.

While in rehab, Carolyn went through the twelve-step program, which helped her to stay sober. It also led her back to church, to God, and to God's authority over her life. Just before her twenty-first birthday, a birthday most people spend getting very drunk, Carolyn made the commitment to a life of sobriety. However, sobriety and acceptance of God in her life still had a few hurdles to overcome.

At twenty-five years old, after five years sober, and approaching the ten-year anniversary of her rape, Carolyn started having flashbacks of that fateful night. The pain and agony that night brought became very real again. Yet this time agony was also met with an awakening in her spirit. Looking at it now, she believes it was a way of God telling her, "I am going to put you back together." She knew she could not handle the flashbacks alone, so Carolyn sought out counseling and was put on psych meds.

She was also using relationships to drown out the pain. She went from one boyfriend to another through her early and mid twenties. None of her boyfriends were abusive, but they were not right for her. By her late twenties, she was done trying to find a husband. She realized that she first needed to be happy with herself and let go of that part of her life. She gave up dating and focused on finishing college.

Carolyn also did something that was reminiscent of ten years prior. She got on her knees and prayed to God. This time she prayed for God to show her the way. Like with Christianity in her youth, Carolyn had checked all the boxes for the twelve-step program. She had successfully completed the program and remained sober. She helped others become sober. People looked up to her, but she still felt horrible. She knew she was missing something, and she needed God to show her the way so she could really feel that change in her life.

At twenty-nine years old, thirteen years after being raped, and eight years sober, Carolyn fully surrendered to Christ. It was when she surrendered, she was able to get off her psych meds no longer having a crutch to drugs (legal or illegal) or alcohol. From that time on she began to see things change drastically in her life.

"Humble yourselves in the sight of the Master, and He shall lift you up" (James 4:10).

On her thirtieth birthday, she met her husband, and for the first time in her entire life she went on a "real first date." God brought Carolyn and her husband into a personal relationship with Him within their first year of marriage. They did not plan to come to God together, but it was a journey that happened simultaneously. They both became dedicated to attending church and were both Baptized. Through regular attendance in church Carolyn began to feel the freedom of releasing her past, and she was able to usher in the wonderful lives of her three sons.

Carolyn feels blessed that God has entrusted her to raise three men and to be able teach them to respect women. Her husband and sons have shown her how she is supposed to be loved. It is their love that has brought more healing to her life. Carolyn admits that she isn't sure if she would be strong enough to raise a daughter. "There is not much more my parents could have done to save me. It only took one night to change my life."

"For every matter there is an appointed time, even a time for every pursuit under the heavens:...a time to heal...a time to be silent, and a time to speak..." (Eccles. 3:1, 3, 7).

For several years, Carolyn has sought out God and understanding. She knows she wasn't being a slut when she was raped. She realizes her youth was stolen from her. The devil had worked in those young men to do the unthinkable. The devil had used them to break her, but in that brokenness a relationship with God has been formed and healing is happening.

During her healing, Carolyn has been drawn to the story of Job, a good man who God allowed Satan to tempt. Carolyn believes that like Job God allowed Satan to work in her life. He allowed that night to happen, and He mourned for her as she mourned when she was raped. However, He knew that the most painful time in her life would be used to redeem her even though Carolyn did not immediately see that. "I'm not sure what I would be like without that happening to me. The brokenness ultimately saved me even though it is still painful twenty years later. This event made me see and realize I needed a savior."

God has used Carolyn as a voice to share the word with athletes. Carolyn has gone on to speak at Fields of Faith and several Fellowship of Christian Athletes events. At the Fields of Faith event, there were about a hundred people. She was very nervous but had the strength to share her story. She understood that her testimony was the strongest weapon God gave her against Satan. No one could debate what God did in her life. It was time for her to use her testimony to glorify Him. She thanked God for putting her out there. It was a surreal experience because as she shared her story God was feeding her scripture. She would cite scripture that she didn't even remember she had read before. It felt like an out of body experience. At the end of her testimony, she felt led to have an altar call which led to salvations. "Every time I share my story, it helps me to heal some. I trust God to use this to help others."

Remember when I asked you what chains you are carrying? Were some of them trauma, addiction, fear, grief, or pain? Carolyn has felt all those chains too. Each time those chains became too strong to bear on her own she cried out. She reached out for help from the Lord. And what did He do? He broke them and helped her begin to heal.

God took what Satan meant for evil, and he turned it into her redemption story. He removed her desire to drink and use drugs. He healed her trauma, so she no longer needed prescription medication. He showed her extraordinary love and sent four guys into her life to give her unconditional love.

Carolyn has realized through God's love that no matter how painful an event, it can be used to strengthen our faith, and that God is always working for our good. God used the pain, destruction, and subsequent healing for Carolyn to minister to both athletes and those struggling with alcoholism. On that fateful night many years ago, God knew that He would use her to transform other people's lives.

Carolyn's message is this: "The redemption and testimony of my life is evidence to me that God is real, and the Gospel is transforming. My life has been transformed. If you're reading this and feel like you're in a dark place with no way out, no hope, I strongly encourage you to call on God. I promise you, He will answer and respond with a love greater than anything you have experienced."

Chapter Seven
You're Never too far Gone

My husband is a very analytical person, so when I try throwing motivational quotes at him he shuts me out. He wants facts. He wants to know how whatever I am saying applies to his life. He wants to know the reason behind the method, the potential outcome, and the estimated success rate. Saying "just because" or "I have a feeling" doesn't work with him. There is definitely a balance we have created between my free-flowing mind and his strict analytics.

Since we have been together for twelve years, married for nine, some of his analytical tendencies have rubbed off on me. (And I'm happy to say some of my free-flowing spirit has rubbed off on him.) Anyway, when I hear the saying "you're never too far gone" as it relates to scripture, my mind goes into analytical mode. Let's be honest: "you're never too far gone" is a very true but heavily used motivational quote that summarizes a large portion of the Bible. What does it truly mean to say, "You're never too far gone?"

To answer the question above we, have to first find out what God considers to be acts that distance ourselves from him.

"These six matters Yahweh hates, and seven are an abomination to Him:

A proud look,
A lying tongue,
And hands shedding innocent blood,
A heart devising wicked schemes,
Feet quick to run to evil,
A false witness breathing out lies,
And one who causes strife among brothers."
(Prov. 6:16–19).

I don't know about you, but I have been guilty of doing a couple of those in my younger years (and I am still far from perfect). In fact, I would think that just about everyone has been a part of spreading rumors (especially with social media) and been prideful at least once. So by these admissions alone it sounds like we all have sinned and come short of the glory of God. Wait a minute. That's in the Bible too!

> *"For all have sinned and fall short of the esteem of*
> *Elohim" (Rom. 3:23).*

Okay so we have established what God hates, and we have established that we have all sinned. What is the consequence of sin and is there a way we can be redeemed from the punishment of sin?

> *"For the wages of sin is death, but the favourable*
> *gift of Elohim is everlasting life in Messiah Yeshua*
> *our Master" (Rom. 6:23).*

God knows we are sinners. He knows that the human spirit is not perfect. He also knows that to sin means death, but God loves us so much that he sent his son to die for us so that our sins may be forgiven.

> "But Elohim proves His own love for us, in that while we were still sinners, Messiah died for us" (Rom. 5:8).

But our sins aren't just forgiven through the blood of Jesus Christ. His death also gave us the opportunity to live for eternity in Heaven. When we accept Jesus as our Lord and Savior our sins are washed clean. It doesn't mean that it never happened. It means that we are made new through Jesus. God no longer sees the sins of our past. He sees the hope for our future.

> "And the favour of our Master was exceedingly increased, with belief and love which are in Messiah Yeshua. Trustworthy is the word and worthy of all acceptance, that Messiah Yeshua came into the world to save sinners, of whom I am foremost. But because of this I received compassion, so that in me first, Yeshua Messiah might display all patience, as an example to those who are going to believe on Him for everlasting life" (1 Tim. 1:14–16).

When you think about your life and the sins you have committed, realize that God has already put everything in place for you to be forgiven. There is no distance you can run from Him nor sin you have committed that He is not willing to reach out for you. He has proven that. It is you who must be willing to prove that you want to come back to Him. This is what it means to say "you are never too far gone."

"Yahweh your Elohim in your midst, is mighty to save. He rejoices over you with joy, He is silent in His love, He rejoices over you with singing" (Zeph. 3:17).

Korry

"And we know that all matters work together for good to those who love Elohim, to those who are called according to His purpose" (Rom. 8:28).

There are times when you meet people and you just click. You immediately become friends and can share personal stories without fear of being judged. That happened when I met Korry. We both started working at a locally owned restaurant within a month of each other, and pretty quickly thereafter we were sharing life stories and cracking jokes.

Korry was very authentic from the beginning. When I introduced myself to her, I asked her how she got the job at the restaurant. She shared with me without pause that she was living at a drug rehabilitation center, and that this was part of the final phase of her time there. They were working on re-introducing her to society and teaching her how to make a living without drugs. I was amazed by her candid nature and willingness to be open.

Over the eight months we worked together, we had many talks about God and her path back to him. Yet nothing could have prepared me for the raw and emotional conversation we had when she gave me the full story for this book.

"I want to share my story because if what I went through can help just one person then it was worth it to me."

Korry and her family moved to America from England when she was in the third grade. She was teased a lot for her accent and for saying things improperly due to the difference in word usage between England and America. Like so many other teen girls Korry never felt like she fit in. She was insecure, and unpopular at school. She was also afraid she would be judged for being herself. While she grew up in a Christian home and was raised in the church, the fear and anxiety were strong enough that she rebelled.

Korry wanted to be able to suppress her dislike for herself, so at fifteen, she turned to weed and alcohol to mask the pain. The pain exceeded those addictions, and she wondered if stronger drugs would hide her feelings. At sixteen, she started using cocaine and crack, and by seventeen she was using meth. Each drug she liked more than the last. Korry thought that she was sneaky with her drug use, but her parents were more aware than she realized. However, they didn't know how long or to what extent Korry was using so they didn't confront her about her drug use.

When Korry was seventeen, she met her soon to be husband. They met while Korry was living at a crack dealer's house. While she was there, the dealer's brother would hang around a lot because he was interested in Korry. He brought his friend over to meet Korry. This friend would become Korry's husband. He was a drug user too, and both were high off and on while they were together.

Korry moved in with her soon to be husband seven days after they started dating. He became verbally abusive after the first month they were together. Korry refused to tell her parents though. They had advised against the relationship, but she wanted to be with him, so Korry didn't listen. When he became abusive, she didn't want the I-told-you-so conversation. After being together for six months, they moved into her parent's house. When she was nineteen, they decided to tie the knot. Four years after getting married Korry found out she was pregnant.

All Korry ever wanted to be was a mom so when she found out she was pregnant she quit all drugs and alcohol cold turkey. She remained sober during her entire pregnancy and through three months of breastfeeding. She even started going to church again.

Going back to church was amazing. Korry hadn't been to church since she was fifteen, but it was like visiting extended family. It was a big positive in her life. Korry's husband even went to church with her.

However, drugs were still around her 24/7, and the craving for the next hit began to pull at her. At four months postpartum, Korry began using drugs again. Her drug use was just as bad as when she quit thirteen months prior. She got back into meth, and her drug use spiraled out of control. This was in part due to the mental abuse her husband was inflicting upon her. Korry's husband would tell her he was the only person who would ever love her, no one would want to deal with her crazy mess, and that she had to have him to be successful.

Shortly after she began to spiral out of control, Korry's parents had to make the incredibly difficult choice of trying to save their daughter whom they loved dearly and had raised or their grandson, an innocent child who truly had no way out on his own. Her parents chose to save their grandson. Her parents knew she didn't want to get sober and had made peace with Korry's choices. They had to wait for her to come back to them, but they knew in order to save their grandson this was the step they had to take.

Losing her son was the hardest thing Korry ever went through. Watching her parents drive away with her son was devastating. She had to trust with all her heart that this was the right choice. While she doesn't remember much of those years, she remembers being scared that something might happen to her son if he stayed with her and his father. She was thankful her parents took her son, and for the once a month visits, she had with him.

Between losing her son and the abuse she received from her husband Korry became suicidal. She only tried to commit suicide once, but it was something she had planned out many times over. Korry had a notebook she would keep with ideas of different ways to kill herself including ways that would be less traumatic for her parents to find her, and ways she wouldn't suffer when she decided to go through with it.

What sent her over the edge from planning to executing was devastation and complete loss of hope. Korry's husband had been verbally abusive for many years but had never put his hands on her in an aggressive way. This time was different though. When her husband laid hands on Korry for the first time, it broke her heart.

He grabbed her by the throat and held her up so that her feet were no longer touching the ground. There were other people in the room, but they did nothing to stop him. When he finally let her go, she left with one of his friends. Korry thought this was a friend that was there to comfort her. Instead the friend gave her Ecstasy, and she committed adultery with him. Korry was so ashamed and mad because she knew that if she had been in her right mind that would have never happened. She always swore that she would never cheat on her husband.

The next day she came back home and told her husband what happened. He drug her outside by her hair and told her she was pathetic and nasty. He turned the fight from the previous day and the adultery into entirely her fault even though he also admitted to committing adultery the night before. After the fight, Korry's husband disappeared for two days. Korry called her parents to let them know that their son shouldn't come over that day.

Korry laid in bed that day and tried to OD on a drug she had been prescribed. She took thirty days' worth in one day. The next day her dad found her. He was able to speak to her counselor who told him that Korry would be fine since she had survived the night. The pills she took were weak enough that Korry would have had to take a much larger amount to have overdosed.

Korry became mad at herself after this. She wasn't mad at herself for trying to kill herself. She was mad because she felt like she couldn't do anything right. She couldn't take care of her son. She couldn't stay faithful to her husband, and she couldn't even kill herself. After that day, Korry's life went into a downward spiral.

Even through the abuse and drug-related arrests, Korry stayed with her husband. She didn't feel like she had anywhere to go. She could only stay at homeless shelters or domestic violence shelters for a couple weeks at a time so she didn't see the point in pursuing those options because she would only end up right back where she was. She got deeper into her drug use during this time. It allowed her to "hunker down" and bear the abuse.

When she was twenty-six, her husband went to prison on a probation violation for a grand theft charge. She was now stuck in the drug life by herself. She didn't stay alone for long. She met another guy who was in the drug scene. The abuse she faced from this man was even worse than her husband.

This man was not a verbal abuser. He was a physical abuser. He took pleasure in torturing Korry. He would burn her with his cigarettes, lock her in the bedroom for days on end, and he popped her eardrums. Again, Korry stayed in this abusive relationship because she felt like she had nowhere to go. She couldn't go to her parents because they were raising her son, and even in that drug induced haze she knew she didn't want the people in her life to be around her son.

During this relationship, Korry had a couple of stints in jail related to drugs. She never tried to fight the charges, so she only spent a couple months in jail at a time. She adapted very well to jail. She wasn't being abused, so it was her "vacation time to build strength." Jail was her safe place. When she got out of jail the last time, her boyfriend was sent to jail. She had anxiety coming out of jail due to not knowing where she would go but was excited at the same time.

She found a place with her next boyfriend. This boyfriend was also abusive, but by this time Korry was done with always being the victim. She became equally abusive to him. She was angry. She took all those years of abuse and unleashed it in what she called a "sick game" they played with each other. They were in a constant state of trying to one up each other.

This was one of the few points in our conversations when I asked Korry if she was willing to explain, and she refused. "It was too sick, and not something that I want to relive." While she still had a very calm demeanor, this was the first time I could see a twinge of pain. But it was also at this point where her life had become so incredibly twisted that she began to feel the desire to end her life in the drug world.

While she didn't notice it at the time, looking back she can see little things happening that she realized she was starting to open back up to God including the last time she was in jail. The last day in jail she said the Lord's Prayer and was determined not to get high when she got out. However, twenty-four hours after being out, her boyfriend beat her, and she got back into drugs. He was soon removed from her life though. Like the previous men in her life, he was sent to jail. The worst was yet to come.

After her last boyfriend went to jail, her second boyfriend got out of jail. He was furious that she had been dating another guy while he was in jail. He decided to sell Korry into sex slavery as a way to pay off his debts.

This was the moment Korry's entire demeanor changed. She became reserved and her face went stone-cold when talking about that time of her life. It was clear that out of all the hell she had been through while living in the drug world, sex slavery was by far the most painful. "I thought I was going to die."

This was the only time Korry ever promised to stop doing drugs. Before this time, Korry would never tell anyone that she would stop doing drugs if they would do something for her. She knew it was a lie because she had no intention of quitting and did not want to manipulate people like that. But this time she meant it. Halfway through her captivity, she prayed to God. She said, "God if you help me survive, I promise I will quit drugs." Shortly after this prayer she saw her opportunity to escape. She took the opportunity and fled from that way of life.

> *"No trial has overtaken you except such as is common to man, and Elohim is trustworthy, who shall not allow you to be tried beyond what you are able, but with the trial shall also make the way of escape, enabling you to bear it"* (1 Cor. 10:13).

When Korry escaped, she got in touch with her parents and asked them to help her get clean. The first place she went to was a faith-based domestic violence shelter. Korry's mom would regularly send her Bible verses to help her keep going. She joined a support group at a church they attended and was able to meet other women who went through similar circumstances as her. They were able to share about how God had helped them. Korry remained sober throughout the program. At thirty years old, fifteen years after she started using drugs, Korry began her journey at a rehabilitation shelter.

At first Korry was reluctant to go to rehab. She was worried she didn't have the right tools to live a sober life. She was worried about things people who have not been in the drug scene would consider normal. How would she find a real job? What would it be like to buy a car or rent an apartment? Even through her reluctancy, she knew she didn't want to go back down the path she had just left.

Korry considers her time in rehab to be her saving grace. Each class she took whether it was finance or forgiveness led back to the Bible. Grief counseling helped her to overcome the trauma she had faced while on drugs. They also taught her to forgive herself. Korry felt immense shame for what she did to her son, family, and for her part in her failed marriage. She realized that hating herself only kept her in her past. Not only did she have to forgive those who hurt her, but also forgive herself for what she did to others. "Jesus forgave me. If He can forgive me, then who am I not to forgive myself."

> "If we confess our sins, He is trustworthy and righteous to forgive us the sins and cleanse us from all unrighteousness" (1 John 1:9).

Going through recovery helped her realize her worth as a child of God. She held on tight to the fact that God gave his only son so she could have eternal life. It was when she realized this that something clicked for her. She began to not be so tough on herself, and for the first time in her life became comfortable with herself.

The rehabilitation program was fifteen months long, and Korry has been out of the program for just over a year. Her mom says Korry is now the person she always knew she could be. Korry's life is the best it has ever been, and it's only getting better.

From the ages of seventeen to thirty, Korry never had to do anything by herself. She always had a man controlling her whether it was finances, rent, car etc. Now she was handling all those on her own, but she was at peace with it. It felt good to be able to do things without someone controlling her. God gave her the strength to handle all the first-time-without-drugs things, like getting her first car, renting her first apartment, etc.

> *"Humble yourselves, then, under the mighty hand of Elohim, so that He exalts you in due time, casting all your worry upon Him, for He is concerned about you"*
> *(1 Pet. 5:6–7).*

Korry has seen many blessings come forth in her life since getting sober. She is finally a happy person, has a good group of people who she can count on, and she has her family back including her son.

At first, she was scared to see her son as they both had trauma from his very early childhood. However, every time they spent time together, she would get more and more excited for the next time. The first weekend he spent the night at her house he rolled over in bed and put his arm on her. She teared up when that happened.

Korry has had to learn her place in his life though because while she is his biological mother, she had not been in his life at all for many years. She is not sad that she doesn't have the traditional mom role yet. She knows that their relationship will continue to grow, and they have lots of fun together. Her son is her biggest reason never to go back to that lifestyle.

Korry's tactics for handling trials have also changed. In the past she would panic, make a rash decision, and turn to drugs. Now she prays about it, has more patience to wait for God's timing, and if she is really nervous, she turns to Christian family and friends to help Biblically guide her.

Korry celebrated three years sober in July 2020. She still attends church and looks forward to where God puts her. Her goal is to become a domestic violence counselor. She wants to be able to help show others that there is life after domestic violence and that there is a way to get out. She hopes to be able to create places where domestic violence victims have more classes and tools to use once they are on their own.

> *"I shall wipe out your transgressions like a cloud, and your sins like a mist. Return to Me, for I shall redeem you"* (Isa. 44:22).

Korry lived half her life in a hellish state filled with excessive drug use, immense emotional trauma, and physical torture. She partook in many of the things that is listed in Proverbs 6:16–19. Yet even with that God still heard her.

He heard her after she spent years of being so high, she didn't know what day it was. He heard her after she was living a life so bad that her son had to be saved from her. He heard her after she decided to no longer be the victim and be equally abusive to her boyfriend. He heard her crying out from her darkest place—alone, tortured through sex slavery. He heard a woman in desperate need for escape and redemption. He heard a woman who was willing to make the change, and He saved her.

He showed her that even with her list of transgressions that she was worth saving. She was worth unconditional love. He showed her that He didn't care about her past sins. He knew that she was made new through the blood of His son, Jesus Christ. Her past transgressions were forgiven.

That is what her family has done too. They have forgiven her. It doesn't mean they have forgotten. It means they do not hold her actions against her and continue to love her for who she is now. Which is what we all should do when faced with a friend or family member who has chosen to turn their life around. Korry's parents knew that she felt shame for what she did to them and her son, but instead of "making her pay" they showed love. They showed joy over her returning to them as the woman they believed she could be.

When I met Korry, I had no idea what her past looked like, and even as I found out bits and pieces it didn't change my opinion of her. I saw a woman who had been through some serious stuff but had made a *huge* turn around. I marveled at the pits of hell she escaped from. I was impressed with her strength and determination. After hearing her full story, I can't wait to see the lives she will change in the future.

Chapter Eight
Forgive Others and Yourself

Forgiveness is an act we should give out easily, but so often we find it hard to accomplish. Why is that? Do we enjoy being mad at others or ourselves? Do we seek retribution? Do we feel like we should constantly beat ourselves up for mistakes made years ago? Do we feel entitled to hold on to anger? While these are yes or no response questions, I understand that there is so much within our society that lurks behind those simple yes or no answers. Let's set aside society, though, and focus on you.

Say you answered yes to any of the questions above. Do you know who ultimately is the biggest victim of your anger and lack of forgiveness? You. Unforgiveness has a negative impact on your life. When you hold unforgiveness in your heart whether it is toward yourself or someone else, you may see relationships disappear, lack of positive movement forward in your life, a continual nagging feeling of depression, anxiety, aggression, etc.

However, once you forgive you begin to see your trials and pain differently. You will be able to look at your life through a lens of positivity. Your life may have changed drastically due to someone's actions, but you will begin to see the good that came from it. You will begin to see how God was working with and for you even during the hard times. You will better understand the lessons that you learned. At times, you may even be thankful for the hardship as it led to a more beautiful future.

When you look at scripture forgiveness is mentioned over and over and over again.

> *"And whenever you stand praying, if you hold what-ever against anyone, forgive, so that your Father in the heavens shall also forgive you your tres-passes" (Mark 11:25).*

> *"Bearing with one another and forgiving each other if anyone has a complaint against another, indeed, as Messiah forgave you so also should you" (Col. 3:13).*

> *"He who covers a transgression seeks love, but he who repeats a matter separates intimate friends" (Prov. 17:9).*

These scriptures (and many more) are why I say forgiveness should be given out easily. God wants us to forgive others. He does not want the spirit of unforgiveness to be in our lives. Even when wrongs are done to us, he wants us to find peace and happiness which many times starts with forgiveness.

Now let's dig deeper into your ability to forgive. Do you freely forgive yourself for mistakes you have made in the past?

There are things that each of us have done in our lives that we are not proud of. Sometimes when we become saved the actions of our past haunt us even more because now, we realize how wrong we were. We pray for forgiveness and in our hearts; we know God has forgiven us. Yet we have a hard time forgiving ourselves. We are our own worst critics after all. So we hold onto the actions of our past letting them interfere with our choices for our future. We move forward, and we are better people than before. Yet there is still that nagging feeling of self-inflicted unforgiveness. Forgiveness doesn't only come from God. You must forgive yourself too.

> *"Not that I have already received, or already been perfected, but I press on, to lay hold of that for which Messiah Yeshua has also laid hold of me. Brothers, I do not count myself to have laid hold of it yet, but only this: forgetting what is behind and reaching out for what lies ahead, I press on toward the goal for the prize of the high calling of Elohim in Messiah Yeshua" (Phil. 3:12–14).*

God releases the chains of eternal bondage, and if you are willing, He can help you release the chains of personal bondage. When we do not forgive ourselves, when we look to the past, and hate ourselves for choices we made, we are not allowing our current selves to progress to better places. Acknowledge your mistakes, learn from them, but do not hold on to them. Let them go.

> *"Because I shall forgive their unrighteousness, and their sins and their lawlessness I shall no longer remember" (Heb. 8:12).*

God wants you to forgive others, and He wants you to forgive yourself as He has forgiven you. He wants you set free from the spirit of unforgiveness. Are you willing to set aside anger and forgive?

"Yahweh is compassionate and showing favour, patient, and great in loving-commitment. He does not always strive, nor maintain it forever. He has not done to us according to our sins, nor rewarded us according to our crookedness. For as the heavens are high above the earth, so great is His loving-commitment toward those who fear Him; as far as the east is from the west, so far has He removed our transgressions from us" (Ps. 103:8–12).

Jim

"And not only this, but we also exult in pressures, knowing that pressure works endurance; and endurance, approvedness; and approvedness expectation" (Rom. 5:3–4).

In the late 1970s, Jim and his best friend, Donnie, walked into a bar after a night at the races and saw that the new bartender, a tall, pretty blonde they had befriended, was working. Jim told Donnie that after he went to the bathroom, he was going to get up the courage to ask the new bartender to go on a date. After returning from the bathroom, he walked up to Donnie who had a big smile on his face. He asked Donnie why he was smiling so much. Donnie told Jim that while he was in the bathroom, he had asked the new bartender to go on a date. She had said yes. Donnie had stolen the girl. Since Donnie was like a big brother to Jim, he didn't get mad, he was happy for him. Little did he know that Donnie and the new bartender would eventually get married and have two daughters, the youngest of which would be me.

I have always known Jim as my dad and mom's best friend. Despite living several states away from each other for most of their adult lives Jim and my dad remained best friends. When my dad passed away twelve years ago, Jim did not let that end his relationship with our family. He had known my mom for thirty years and had watched my sister and I grow up. He continues to check in on all of us regularly.

Jim was one of the first people who came to mind when God told me to write this book. I know what Jim has been like over the years. He is one of the nicest people you will ever meet and is the type of person to always help those in need. However, I knew that if he was my dad's best friend back in the '70s, he'd had a wild streak in his younger years. I had no idea the amount of spiritual transformation Jim had undergone.

Jim was born into a life of instability. He was conceived through adultery and had seven "dads" before he was twelve. When all the other kids had their dads sitting in the bleachers at their baseball games, Jim had no one. Jim and his mother also had a very strained relationship. Jim suffered from severe acne many times having to have mild surgery. He would face excruciating pain during surgery, but his mother didn't care or even acknowledge his pain. Throughout his childhood, she would leave the house telling him she was going to see one of her ex-husbands, and she would come home "with a smile and cigarettes." Even at a young age, Jim knew what was happening. He did not trust her or any of the dads he had except dad number five.

Frank was dad number five. He taught Jim right from wrong, how to hunt and fish, and attended Jim's baseball games. Life was good when Frank was around, but it did not last. Just like husbands one through four, Jim's mother and Frank divorced. Jim wanted to keep the relationship he had with Frank, but his mother moved them away from her ex-husband. After her divorce from Frank, Jim and his mother's relationship all but ceased to exist.

Jim and his mother were looked down upon for the divorces. This was during a time when the divorce rate was very low. They faced judgement from adults and children alike. Adults would treat Jim and his mom differently or comment negatively about their lifestyle. Even the cashier at the grocery store would make comments about their use of food stamps. Kids at school would ask Jim what was wrong with him or call him names because he didn't have a dad.

When you look at someone else's life you only see pieces of the whole. You don't see what they are dealing with in private. You don't see their past that negatively impacted their present. You don't see the internal battles they may be facing. "And do not judge, and you shall not be judged at all. Condemn not, and you shall not be condemned at all. Forgive, and you shall be forgiven" (Luke 6:37). When you allow yourself to be judgmental you are not showing the love of God, and placing a negative burden upon yourself. "He who is without sin among you, let him be the first to throw a stone at her" (John 8:7). While you may not agree with someone's choices, that does not give you the right to judge them. We have all made choices that others may see as questionable. We must not get so righteous in our Christianity that we forget what it felt like prior to us accepting Christ as our Lord and Savior. We need to take into consideration that the person we are judging is on their own journey and may need someone to show them the love of Christ just as we did. There is hypocrisy in a judgmental Christian. "And why do you look at the splinter in your brother's eye, but do not notice the plank in your own eye?" (Matt. 7:3). Do not fall into that trap. Continue to seek the word of God and show others the love that he has shown you.

By the age of thirteen, Jim had started using acid and anything else that would help him forget. He wanted to block out the pain in his life. He became who he hung out with, and his friends became his suppliers.

When he was in high school, he was considered "the ugliest kid in school." He had really bad pimples and was taunted by his classmates. He ended up having to be one of the toughest kids in school. Instead of going to an adult over their bullying, he would fight the kids who made fun of him. The fights got him kicked out of school on occasion, but the taunting subsided some as most people in the school did not want to fight him.

When he was in tenth grade, Jim had a class project that required him to speak in front of the class. He hated speaking in front of people because he knew it would eventually lead to them whispering about his appearance. The thing was though Jim had a great speech written for his class but kept telling his teacher he didn't do it so he wouldn't have to speak in front of everyone. The final day for the assignment Jim's teacher forced him to speak in front of the class. Jim only got a couple sentences into his speech before he saw his classmates starting to whisper. The whispering continued and Jim began to get incredibly frustrated and self-conscious. Jim eventually got mad and threw his homework in his teachers face. He walked out of class and went outside to get high. That was the last day Jim ever went to school.

Your words have power. When you speak you must be wise with your words. Before you speak to someone, think about if what you are saying will have a positive or negative impact. Is what you are getting ready to say even necessary? Do not underestimate the significance your words may have. Someone may only hear you speak once, but once may be enough to set them on a different path. Not only do your words have the power to change someone else's life, but they also show what is in your heart. "But what comes out of the mouth comes from the heart, and these defile the man" (Matt. 15:18). And if you don't care about the impact or feel you should be able to express yourself regardless, you need to take a look at yourself. Being unapologetic and willing to speak negatively to others shows a sadness and bitterness within you. "But Yahweh said to Samuel, 'Do not look at his appearance or at the height of his stature, because I have refused him, for not as man sees, for man looks at the eyes, but Yahweh looks at the heart'" (1 Sam. 16:7).

God judges us by our hearts. He is not someone you can conceal your heart against either. "For the Word of Elohim is living, and working, and sharper than any two-edged sword, cutting through even to the dividing of being and spirit, and of joints and marrow, and able to judge the thoughts and intentions of the heart. And there is no creature hidden from His sight, but all are naked and laid bare before the eyes of Him with whom is our account" (Heb. 4:12–13). Be mindful of your words. Use them to bring others hope, love, and positivity.

You might wonder what Jim's mom thought of him dropping out. She didn't even know. By the time he was fifteen, Jim only came home once a month. He would spend his nights partying with friends and sleeping on whatever couch was available. He had no relationship with his mom.

By sixteen, Jim had included alcohol into the mix and became both a drug addict and an alcoholic. He was caught once for possession, but only had 9/10 the amount needed for an arrest, so he was let go. He attempted rehab twice and AA once but left before the thirty days were up.

Jim had zero interest in God and wanted desperately to "accidentally" overdose so he could die. He never purposefully tried to overdose though because part of him knew that it would get better. He just needed more time for things to take care of themselves.

At seventeen, Jim decided he wanted to try to live, and realized he needed discipline, so he joined the Army. He was happier in the Army than in civilian life, but his addiction followed him. Five and a half months into being in the Army, Jim was with some of his Army buddies and got high. A captain approached the group, and firmly grabbed Jim on the shoulder. Thinking it was one of his buddies, Jim turned around and, without looking to see who it was, punched the captain. He immediately started apologizing because he knew what this could mean. He did not want to be kicked out of the Army. He had finally started feeling a sense of belonging. He continued to apologize profusely to the captain, but the damage was done. Jim was discharged from the Army. The officers who discharged him took some pity on him, because they could tell he felt bad about his choice. They did not put a dishonorable discharge on his record, but the discharge they wrote up still blocked him from receiving any veteran's benefits.

Jim had reached a new low. Now he couldn't blame his mom or his "dads" for his circumstances. He had failed. Even with hitting a new low, something had changed in Jim. He had more of a will to live. Jim continued to use drugs and drink, but he shied away from hard drugs. Weed and beer become the substances of choice. Jim also cut off his relationship with his mom completely which relieved a lot of pain from his life.

There are times when, despite the relationship, you have to remove people from your life in order to move forward. God does not want you in a constant state of depression and pain so you can keep a relationship with a family member. "Let all bitterness, and wrath, and displeasure, and uproar, and slander be put away from you, along with all evil" (Eph. 4:31). And while He doesn't want you burdened by their horrible actions, he also doesn't want you burdened by unforgiveness.

"Then Peter came to Him and said, 'Master, how often shall my brother sin against me, and I forgive him? Up to seven times seven?' Yeshua said to him, 'I do not say to you, up to seven times, but up to seventy times seven'" (Matt. 18:21–22). Forgive those who have done wrong by you, but also understand there is a time you may need to remove them from your life.

When he was nineteen, Jim was at a wedding for a marriage he didn't want to be entering into. He didn't even remember how it had gotten to this point. Jim left just before the ceremony started to go to a bar to get drunk. He told everyone at the bar it was his birthday (which it was), that he was getting married, and that he didn't want to get married. The drinks started flowing. My dad, who was the best man, came to the bar to get Jim. He told Jim he couldn't leave her at the altar. Jim returned to the wedding and married the woman. He was so drunk during the ceremony and reception that he didn't remember any of it. One year later the marriage ended in divorce.

Jim was so happy to be out of that marriage. He was ready to have fun. He began seeing a bunch of women with no commitment to any of them. He didn't have a care in the world or any thoughts of God. This carefree lifestyle continued for three years before he met his second wife.

Jim met his second wife in a bar. They played pool together when they first met, and she beat him. Afterward, Jim asked if he could take her out on a date. They both got drunk, and the night ended without much memory due to intoxication. Jim had fun with her though. They partied together for a while, but as things began to get more serious Jim started to slow down.

Jim realized he was tired of being alone. They both had good jobs which added to a level of stability he had not been a part of before, and he thought he was in love. Jim became a married man again. He moved out of the old-fashioned hotel he had lived in and bought a trailer, which they both moved into after they were married.

Jim and his second wife were married for sixteen years and had two daughters together. They had a rocky relationship. Even though Jim had to fight people when he was a kid, he didn't like to argue as an adult. He would have been more than happy to never have to argue, but his wife had a different point of view. Jim and his wife were not a team. They had very different opinions quite often throughout their marriage.

To combat the frustration in his life, Jim focused on his daughters. He tried to do whatever he could so they could have a normal upbringing. Unlike in his life, he wanted his girls to know they always had a dad. He made sure he was the dad he never had.

While their relationship was not perfect, and Jim continued to drink, he remained faithful to his wife. She did not. She cheated on him numerous times. Each time Jim forgave her but did not make that forgiveness known. He continued to try to work on the relationship. However, after years of unfaithfulness, Jim couldn't keep forgiving her. Jim was done. He did not wish ill upon her, but he was done trying to make things better. They divorced shortly thereafter.

Jim was devastated that he was not going to be able to be with his daughters every day. What made matters worse was his ex-wife and her new partner were moving them and the girls several hours away. It didn't stop Jim though from calling his daughters regularly and taking full advantage of joint custody. He cried every time he had to take the girls back to their mother. When his ex-wife had his daughters, he felt like he could not exist. He would barely eat, work eleven to thirteen hours a day, go to the bar until two in the morning, sleep for two to three hours, and repeat the process the next day. There was an end to this destructive path though.

Within a year of their separation, his ex-wife was diagnosed with cancer and passed away. Jim was saddened for his daughters that they lost their mother. He understood that they had gone through a very difficult time at a young age. The empathy he felt for his daughters was matched with personal elation. He was incredibly thankful to be able to be a bigger part of their life again.

Prior to his ex-wife's passing, Jim began to open up to God. For the first time, Jim prayed to God. Jim prayed about the kind of woman he wanted in his life. He wanted someone who was trust-worthy, someone who would show him real love, and someone who didn't lie to him or his daughters. He wasn't going to get married again until he met that woman.

Jim would meet the woman who would become his third wife shortly after his prayer and prior to his ex-wife's passing. He met her around town. After seeing her a couple times and chatting with her, he asked her out on a date. He was nervous for their first date, and almost backed out. Ironically, she was also nervous and almost backed out. However, they both showed up for dinner despite their nerves. They had only talked for five minutes when Jim began having feelings for her. He knew she was the one he had prayed for. He felt like he could trust her. After what Jim had been through with his second wife, trust was a huge positive for him. One year after their first date they were married.

Jim began to notice God working in his life after he met his third wife. The night of his bachelor party Jim got incredibly drunk. He was so drunk that his fiancé had to come pick him up from the bar in the middle of the night. She was furious. She told Jim that she would leave him if he ever did anything like that again.

After they were married Jim would still go out to the bar, but he would not get drunk. He began to not go to the bar for days, then weeks, and eventually was led away from the bar all together.

The same thing happened with smoking. When his wife became pregnant with their daughter, she told Jim he was not allowed to smoke in the house. He obliged and took his smoking outside. One day, his oldest daughter (from the marriage with his second wife) came home from school while he was outside smoking. She was frustrated about something with school and told Jim she couldn't do it. Jim took his cigarette, flicked it out, and said, "I will quit smoking, and you won't say 'I can't' anymore, because if I can quit smoking, you can accomplish what you need to as well." Jim wore a patch for two days, took the patch off on day three, and has not smoked a day since. That was eighteen years ago.

Within a very short period of time, Jim had let go of his addiction to smoking and alcohol. He was the happiest he had ever been, and for the first time in his life he was truly in love with his spouse. Jim's marriage with his third wife was a stark contrast from his relationship with his second wife. While Jim and his wife don't always agree on everything or may get agitated, none of their disagreements have led to a fight or raised voices. "We may see night and day on some things, but we compromise and meet at noon."

Jim took this opportunity to talk to his two oldest daughters about relationships. He never put down his ex-wife, but he did try to teach his girls that healthy relationships did not include yelling at each other every day. Healthy relationships included teamwork, compromise, and good communication.

Three years after Jim quit smoking, he had a heart attack. This was Jim's first slap of reality telling him he wasn't invincible. It also began his continual pursuit of God and helping others.

Jim had a dream that he was at a church standing next to a statue that was in the middle of the square. It was bitterly cold out. He looked up slightly and his body began to turn. He was not moving his feet. It was almost like he was standing on a rotating disc. As he was turning, he began to feel hopeless, hungry and like he was going to lose his mind. This dream gnawed at him for about a week. He couldn't get over the feelings of hopelessness and hunger.

Prior to the dream, Jim served as an alderman for the county he lived in. Through this position he met lots of business owners and people from the community. He decided that he would use his connections to feed the hungry. People at first were surprised by his initiative as there wasn't anything like that in the community, but they began believing in him. Jim helped to organize three potlucks, which fed over a hundred people.

It was also through his connections that he found the church from his dream. The building was failing, and the congregation was small, but the church was situated in a good location for the potlucks. Jim started a soup kitchen at the church. Both the church and the soup kitchen thrived (and continue to thrive). Jim and the church helped each other and the community. Thousands have been fed through the efforts put forth by Jim and the volunteers he worked with.

Jim took a look at his life. He was amazed at how God had timed placing the people he needed in his life as well as the events that led him to that moment. Meeting and marrying his third wife got him on a straighter path. His heart attack helped him to realize he wasn't invincible and started his journey of pursuing God. He became an alderman which allowed him to meet many people within the county. This led to Jim being able to have the resources available to start the soup kitchen.

One year after the soup kitchen was started, Jim had to have both knees replaced. This loss of mobility eventually led to loss of employment and loss of their home. Jim looked at these losses with an open mind and heart to God. He knew that when God closed one door, he was opening another. He knew he had to be patient for God's timing. He also knew that he was not going to live in the valley forever. He was going to look for the best expecting to climb back up.

> *"'Have I not commanded you? Be strong and cou-rageous. Do not be afraid, nor be discouraged, for Yahweh your Elohim is with you wherever you go.' And Joshua commanded the officers of the people, saying, 'Pass through the midst of the camp and command the people, saying, "Prepare food for yourselves, for within three days you are passing over this Jordan, to go in to possess the land which Yahweh your Elohim is giving you to possess'"* (Josh. 1:9–11).

God does not intend for you to endlessly wander through the valley. He has a place that has been secured just for you as a child of God. While the children of Israel wandered for forty years, God knew where He ultimately would take them. They just had to come to Him first. Once they came to Him, God provided the means and ability to move into the Promise Land. Do not become bogged down within the valley. You must continue to pass through the valley in order to get to God's promise. God wants to bless you abundantly, but you have to be willing to accept him, be patient, and understand it is still within His timing.

> *"And you shall love Yahweh your Elohim with all your heart, and with all your being, and with all your might... And it shall be, when Yahweh your Elohim brings you into the land of which He swore to your fathers, to Abraham, to Isaac, and to Jacob,*

to give you great and good cities which you did
not build, and houses filled with all kinds of goods,
which you did not fill, and wells dug which you
did not dig, vineyards and olive trees which you
did not plant, and you shall eat and be satisfied"
(Deut. 6:5, 10–11).

Jim learned that every up and down led to the next. Once he realized that, life became simpler. He had peace in knowing that God was in control of his life, and that he was given opportunities to learn from what was happening in his life. Growing up he had no guidance. No one told him what he could be. It was just him. He is thankful God gave him the ability to choose how to shape his future.

Jim has taken this lesson from his past and turned it into a passion for his present, as he tries to help young people find their direction. He will use everyday interactions to speak with young adults and share what he has learned through God. He likes to tell them to go for a walk. Go back one year and think about where you were. Go back five years and think about where you were. Then, look at where you are now. What plans can you create to make a positive change? He also lets them know that if they are going through a bad spot it's not going to stay bad. He helps them to look at things in a more positive light.

Jim has also found a way to give back to veterans. Recently, Jim began helping veterans at nursing homes. He brings them gifts on holidays and spends time with them just listening to them talk. He likes to ask them one question and then be silent. They will reminisce all day long. When they begin to slow down, he will ask them another question, and they will take off with their story. He loves the look they have on their face while they tell their stories. He also buys meals for veterans when he sees them eating out, and whenever he sees a hat on a veteran, he shakes their hand and thanks them for their service. This is a trait he has passed on to all three of his daughters. Through his work with veterans and the soup kitchen Jim has felt a sense of fulfillment he has never felt before.

Prior to God Jim was a wanderer, focused on the what ifs, and constantly wondering about the future. He felt like he had no direction or reason for existing. Since he accepted God into his life, Jim feels like he has purpose, he has a calm about himself, and feels like he is doing something right. Even with having two heart attacks he has been at peace during those moments and knows he and his family are taken care of.

God is not only physically and emotionally taking care of Jim. He is also making Jim's dreams come true. All of Jim's life he has loved fishing and has always wanted to live on or near a body of water. He grew up fishing on the Mississippi River and has fond memories of the area. After Jim's knee surgery where he lost his home, Jim and his family had to move to a trailer park. They have lived there for six years and just recently have been able to look for a more permanent home. Jim and his wife have looked and looked to no avail until September 2020. Jim's wife decided to look for a home in an area they had yet to look. They found a home on the river that was move-in ready, open floor plan, within their budget, and has a neighbor who is a commercial fisherman. Jim's lifelong prayer to live near a body of water was answered. He also found out his new neighbor's prayer had been answered too. Jim's new neighbor had been praying for a neighbor that enjoyed fishing because he was tired of talking to the fish while fishing. Jim and his family moved into their dream home in October 2020.

Jim believes that he is living proof that you have a choice in life, and you can't do it by yourself. He knows that God has a purpose for him. We are chosen to be here at this time for a reason. Jim so beautifully put it that we are given a soul once. When we are fulfilled with His intention then we become part of the light.

> *"For you were once darkness, but now you are light*
> *in the Master. Walk as children of light" (Eph. 5:8).*

Jim's life has been dotted by people who played an important role in his life that abused him mentally, judged him, lied to him, and hurt him. Jim also made decisions that negatively impacted his life. Jim has lived a life that needs to be filled with forgiveness.

I asked Jim if he forgave his mother or second wife for the pain they inflicted upon his life. He responded that he had not forgiven his second wife, but he had forgiven his mother a couple years ago. Yet doesn't know how heartfelt that forgiveness was. When I asked him if he forgave himself for his actions, he immediately responded yes.

Jim's response, I felt, brought beautiful, honest truth to this chapter. Forgiveness is an act we should give out easily, but so often we find it hard to accomplish. Jim, like all of us, is human. He felt and still feels real pain for what happened to him. Jim has wanted to have some semblance of forgiveness, but his heart still feels anger. Those who have hurt him have either passed on or moved on/forgotten their part in his pain. Who is hurting from this unforgiveness? Him.

Jim has done God's work feeding the hungry and showing love to the veterans. He now needs to ask God to work on him. Jim needs to open up to God and ask for peace from his past, and to settle his angry heart through forgiveness. When he does that he will truly be at peace with his past and be able to move on with his future.

"Do not remember the former events, nor consider the events of old" *(Isa. 43:18).*

Chapter Nine
Strength, Happiness, and Peace

My husband and I have three daughters, all of which were born within five years of each other. We are constantly amazed at both the similarities and differences in our daughters. Seeing them come into their personalities is one of our favorite (and sometimes most stressful) moments. When I think of each daughter, there is a certain quality about them that stands out and has stood out about each of them since birth.

My oldest daughter is strength. When I have my I'm-failing-as-a-mom moments, she can sense my silent frustration. I don't have to say a word. She just knows. She will walk up to me, wrap her beautiful little arms around me and just hug the frustration out of me. She will then give me a kiss and ask what she can help me with. She has done this since she could walk and talk at two years old. God truly blessed me with an incredible first-born child.

My middle daughter is happiness. Since she was an infant, this child has made the silliest faces to make others laugh. When she was one to two years old, she would walk into a room and just start laughing. There didn't have to be anything going on in the room. She would just laugh which would then make you laugh. She is quirky and has a light about her. Whenever I have had a long day, I can always count on her to make me smile.

My youngest daughter is peace. While she definitely makes her voice heard now, she is still the most peaceful child. She is the calm when my two oldest are being stormy. When either of her older sisters are crying, she gives them hugs, kisses them and snuggles them until they calm down. She loves comforting people, and her laughs can release all tension from the room.

While each of our daughters have many more amazing attributes, I find it incredible that the ones that stand out the most are strength, happiness and peace because when I accepted God into my life, I found those things as well. I look at my daughters as His physical reminder to me of what He has done in my life.

When speaking with each person for this book, I asked them how their life has changed since accepting God. They each gave specific examples, but there were three overarching commonalities between everyone: strength, happiness, and peace. In a world filled with fear, anger and turmoil, God gave them the strength to overcome fear, happiness to outshine the anger, and peace to lay siege to the turmoil. God gave each of them the tools they needed to live wonderful lives.

> *"Peace I leave with you, My peace I give to you. I do not give to you as the world gives. Do not let your heart be troubled, neither let it be afraid"* (John 14:27).

Warren

> *"And Yeshua said to them, 'Come, follow Me, and I shall make you become fishers of men'"* (Mark 1:17).

When I felt the need to be challenged spiritually, God led myself and my family to the church we are in now. The church is much larger than other churches we have attended so it took time to meet many of the people we know now. About three months after we started going to the church, I joined the Prayer Team. Warren is the Prayer Team leader.

I was already several interviews into the book when I approached Warren about his story. Warren had actually been placed on my heart for almost a month before I asked him if he would be willing to share his story. The silly thing about it was I was still nervous to ask people to be in the book. I knew this was what God had assigned me to do but asking people that I didn't know very well to share their life's story with me was still nerve wracking. God made sure I listened to Him though.

One night after getting out of the Prayer Center, Warren and I happened to get into an extended conversation. While Warren and I had talked plenty since being on the Prayer Team together, it had always been in short bursts just before the phone lines opened or in between calls. But that night we happened to start talking afterward, and we just kept talking. We talked some about him going to school for ministry, how God has been working in each of our lives, leadership, accountability etc. During this conversation I knew what God was doing. At this point, I was keeping the book under wraps and hadn't wanted to ask Warren in front of other people. Mostly because I wasn't asking them to be in the book, and I didn't want to seem rude. It's like God was saying, "Here is your opportunity, Sarah. No one else is around. Ask Warren to be in the book." I literally waited until just before saying our goodbyes to ask.

While I was asking Warren to be in the book, I was mentally scolding myself for almost letting fear get the best of me. I was also silently thanking God for giving me enough courage (and ample opportunity) to ask Warren to share his story.

When Warren was in school, he was satisfied with being able to get a *C* in his schoolwork. He did not seek to excel in education or the sports that he played. He was fine with just doing enough to get by. That is how he lived much of his adult life as well until he fully allowed God into his life.

Growing up, Warren always felt like the square peg trying to be placed in a round hole. However, he would do whatever he needed so he would feel like he fit in including smoking pot, drinking, and eventually using cocaine. Even when he was living with his parents, they did not reprimand him when he went against their teachings. Warren can see even now how, at times, their unwillingness to reprimand or allow Warren to face the consequences of his actions enabled him to go further down the path of addiction even though they did not know of his drug addiction until he was nine months sober. When there are no consequences for poor behavior it can make that behavior even easier to do.

> *"And indeed, no discipline seems pleasant at the time, but grievous, but afterward it yields the peaceable fruit of righteousness to those who have been trained by it" (Heb. 12:11).*

While he grew up in a Christian home, he was taught religion and not about having a relationship with God. Not only did he rebel against his parents, but he also rebelled against God. Warren eliminated God from his life, and he felt no shame for his actions and their negative impacts on others. Warren felt like he was God. His life was all about himself. He would do whatever he needed to do to take care of himself.

When Warren was eighteen, he joined the Army, despite his mom asking him not to. At the time, the job market was so bad, the Army seemed like a much better option. Warren did not use drugs or drink alcohol for the effect. He did it to fit in socially so the impact it had on his performance in the military was minimal. During the military it was almost like Warren went into remission as his priorities switched. He gave 100 percent of himself to serving. He could run six-minute miles and jump out of airplanes. However, his attitude of superiority grew, and he had the mentality that he would run over anyone that got in his way. This hothead attitude would prove to be a major downfall in his life.

When President Jimmy Carter passed the Affirmative Action bill, Warren was passed up for a promotion that he had earned. Warren was furious. He was also up for reenlistment. Warren chose not to reenlist. He hated the Army and burned his uniform once he was discharged. Warren would face a hurdle that many former military personnel face, even today. He didn't know how to be a civilian.

His addiction came back with a vengeance. This time it wasn't just social drug and alcohol use. Now Warren was drinking to take him out of himself. He had planned on doing twenty years in the military and going to Korea. Now none of that was happening, and he didn't know how to cope. He blamed the military for the state of his life.

> *"The foolishness of man perverts his way, and his heart is wroth against Yahweh" (Prov. 19:3).*

Warren didn't reevaluate his life when he was discharged from the Army. He just moved on to the next job which was being a prison guard. He continued to go bar hopping, chasing women, and using cocaine. He went through relationships like they meant nothing and did not care about the feelings of the woman who he was involved with. His partying ways eventually caught up with him. Warren was caught trespassing. When the cop approached him, he was defiant, and in his drunken stupor, he made ter-roristic threats. He ended up in jail with the people he guarded. There was no forgiveness from his job. They asked him to resign, or he would be fired.

From twenty-three to thirty-six years old, Warren lived his life on repeat: eat-drink-smoke-sleep, with work thrown in between. His weed usage increased, but he did not realize his addiction was getting worse. Warren did begin to realize he had no inner peace, no hope, and no faith. Yet it would still take years before Warren would feel ashamed for his actions and recognize that he was out of control.

Warren would live a life of stark contrasts from thirty-six to forty-six years old. On Saturday nights, he would be drunk, singing in bars, but on Sundays, he would be singing in the church choir. He would also receive three DUIs during this time period. Once at thirty-six years old, another at thirty-seven years old, and the final at forty-six years old.

It was during this time that the pastor at the church Warren was attending approached Warren and told him he needed to hang out with more church people. Warren was confused as he did spend time with people from the church. The pastor clarified. He told Warren that he needed to hang out with people who had battled what Warren was battling and knew that God was the way to recovery. In the midst of those ten years, though, Warren did not want to hear those words. He had not yet gotten to the point where he felt like he needed to change his way of thinking.

In 2005, Warren would receive his final DUI, which racked up $60,000 in fines and lawyer bills. He took a look at his life and realized that he had wasted most of his time and income (approx-imately $30,000 a year) on drugs, alcohol, and the repercussions of his addiction. He had three marriages (and would eventually have four) that ended due to alcohol and drug use. He finally understood that he needed to let God come into his life to help relieve himself of the obsession with drugs and alcohol. Warren knew he had to have faith and that God would restore him.

Warren began his road to recovery by joining Alcoholics Anonymous. In AA, Warren learned he was not the victim. He didn't drink because of everyone else. He chose to drink. He began to recognize his part in his addiction and stopped blaming others for his actions. It was a great stepping point, but he knew God wanted him to do more.

So in October of 2005, Warren entered rehab. The facility he was in had ten beds and ten doctors, so he was incredibly fortunate to receive one on one care. He began to learn that it was okay not to drink, and that it was okay to not be okay. It began to click for Warren that God could help him overcome the things he'd always struggled with. God could do for him what he couldn't do for himself. He prayed for God to restore and release him from his obsession.

> *"Cast your burden on Yahweh and let Him sustain you; He never allows the righteous to be shaken"*
> *(Ps. 55:22).*

Warren began to feel hope. He realized that through God he could live a life beyond his wildest dreams. He understood that God is a higher power and began to rely more on God than man. He also began to have the courage to move on with his life without the addictions.

Warren achieved sobriety on October 25, 2005. Seeing a neon light no longer triggered him to drink. Seeing people drinking no longer made him want to drink. Warren understood that while he had changed others he knew may not have. Many of Warren's former drinking/drug buddies disappeared. However, a couple drinking buddies did stick around. One of which asks Warren to pray for him occasionally. Warren wanted to live his life in a straight line, so he made the adjustments in his life and routine.

Three years after becoming sober, Warren decided to move to Florida. His sobriety wouldn't fail, but the move would create an eight-year hiatus from attending church. Warren had yet to learn the difference between religion and a relationship with God. He began to create excuses as to why he couldn't go to church when others would talk to him about attending church. One of his excuses was that the bass tournaments he participated in were on Sundays.

One such instance happened while Warren was at the gym. He met a man who attended a church near where Warren lived. He invited Warren to attend. Warren wasn't opposed to the offer. Afterall, through his time in rehab Warren had opened up more to God, but he still created excuses. God wasn't going to let Warren get off that easy though.

About a year later, Warren (who had been a postal worker since he'd resigned from being a prison guard) noticed that he recognized one of the names on his mail route. It was the pastor of the church that the man at the gym had invited him to. Warren had heard in his years of learning religion about watching for signs and wonders. He took the pastor being on his mail route as a sign. He was open and had a willingness to change so he decided to act on the invitation to attend church.

Attending that church changed the way Warren looked at life. He listened to the pastor about being faithful, believing, and tithing. In 2017, Warren began to have a personal relationship with God. When he opened up to God, he felt mind-blowing relief, and everything in his life shifted. Everything he had been looking for in his life, the things he always felt were missing relationally, he found in God. He felt hope and knew God had restored his life.

Warren realized the life he had dreamed he would live when he became sober twelve years prior was happening and then some. He was living a life beyond his wildest dreams.

Even how Warren looked at trials in his life changed drastically. He no longer instantaneously reacted. He would step back, ask God for guidance, and then rationally respond to the situation. God was giving him wisdom on how to better handle situations that, in his past, would have been difficult to overcome. With his change in heart, he realized that he needed to be careful with his actions because he is a reflection of God.

Miracles were happening in his life as well. At fifty-eight, he was able to buy his first home just before retiring. He was supposed to see three different houses one day with a realtor. He knew the first house was the one. It was the biggest, nicest house he had ever looked at. He and his parents prayed over the house, and within forty-three days, he owned the house. This house gave him the ability to have his parents who were in their early to late eighties to live with him.

He has been able to build a relationship with them that he did not have during his years of addiction and has been able to take care of them as they have progressed in years. His parents are proud of the man he has become and are thankful that they can enjoy this time with him.

At sixty, Warren felt the calling to attend Bible college. His days of "just getting by" in school are far from over, and he will receive cum laude honors when he graduates from college this year.

When Warren was an alcoholic and addicted to cocaine, his parents did not trust him to do the right thing, and his friends did not turn to him for advice. Since accepting God into his life, not only does he care for his parents who live with him, but others seek out Warren for advice. People now call Warren truthful and respectful. Those are two words that Warren never thought people would use to describe him. Having a relationship with God has changed Warren's life and gave him renewed strength, happiness, and peace. "Without Him, I would be nothing."

> *"Yah is my strength and song, and He has become*
> *my deliverance. He is my El, and I praise Him—*
> *Elohim of my father, and I exalt Him" (Exod. 15:2).*

Warren's story is a beautiful testament to the fact that God does not care about your age. He does not care if you have lived twenty or fifty years without Him. His love knows no time. He listens for the time that you call out for Him. When Warren decided he needed help, God came to his aid. He placed people and resources in Warren's life to help him overcome addiction, and to return Warren to the church. Even the church God placed Warren in helped Warren to grow in his faith to the extent of wanting to spread the word himself.

God is a warrior. He will fight with you and for you. He will remove strongholds of addiction, fear and pain. He will replace them with strength, happiness, and peace. God fought for Warren when he felt weak and showed him a new way of life.

Work in Progress

There are hundreds of instances during the process of writing this book that I was amazed by these individuals who bore their souls. However, one of the things that I thought was incredibly beautiful about each was their understanding that they are still a work in progress. They don't claim to be perfect or know all the answers. They all know that as long as they are on this earth, they will make mistakes, but that they have been redeemed through Christ Jesus. They appreciate that they are a work in progress and that God will continue to mold them.

One of the questions I asked every person who contributed to this book was "What advice would you like to give to the reader?" While each of their stories are incredibly powerful, I wanted them to be able to have a chance to share from the place they are now in their life vs their past.

"Listen to counsel and accept discipline, so that you are wise in your latter end" (Prov. 19:20)

Advice from Carolyn

The purpose of the cross is for pain and sin. Take your pain and put it at the cross. It is all washed away when you accept Christ. It is a process, and you need to be patient. Understand that life is not perfect.

Advice from Frank

Never try to find your worth in man or rely on man. Find your worth through Christ. Let him into your life. You become worthy through God.

Advice from Jennifer

Pick up the Bible even if you don't understand it. God will plant the seed of understanding. When you struggle, pick a verse to stand on. When you make decisions in life don't just think about how you feel now. Think about how your future self may feel about what you are doing. Make choices that your future self will be proud of.

Advice from Jim

What have you done so far? What is your attitude like? What do you think about at night? Do you think life could be better? If you think things haven't gone well so far, and you think you need help, start trusting God.

Advice from Korry

Love God with your whole heart. If you trust in Him, He will be whatever you are needing: a comforter, a provider, a father or a best friend. He is all you need to feel complete.

Advice from Rachel

You are never too far gone—never too lost to be found. Never feel unworthy or unloved. Know that Christ lives within us. He makes us worthy.

Advice from Randall

Try to really get to know God. Do not rely on others to tell you what you should think. Get into the Bible yourself, read the

Gospels and *know* the God you love. Know that once you accept God into your life you become a target for Satan. He will use everything to distract you. Take your walk with God seriously so that you are living a life that reflects Him.

Advice from Sam

It is never too late to accept Christ. Through your darkest times you are not alone; God will carry you. God always knows your journey and the end of your story. Let Him give you the vision that you can have more.

Advice from Stephanie

Spend time alone with God. Remove all distractions and communicate with Him. One on one time with God can alter your life. Do not get caught up in the checklist of going to church and reading your Bible. When you feel it has become a checklist, get back to basics. Be excited about spending time with God.

Advice from Warren

God gives you wisdom to handle situations. Use the wisdom given to you, trust in the Lord, and He will take you out of the pits of hell. He has the hope that we look for. With God all things are possible.

> *"Not to us, O Yahweh, not to us, but to Your Name give esteem, for your loving-commitment, for your truth... You who fear Yahweh, trust in Yahweh; He is their help and their shield. Yahweh has remembered us; He blesses us... Yahweh gives you increase more and more, you and your children. You are blessed by Yahweh, who made the heavens and earth" (Ps. 115: 1, 11–12, 14–15).*

Reflection and Salvation

My husband and I were married when I was twenty-four, and at that time I was rather against church and organized religion. The only request my husband had for our wedding though was to have the wedding be officiated by his childhood pastor. I had no problem with that because I had never gone to church as a kid, teen, or twenty-year-old. This was also before people got married in barns, so I didn't have a location or officiant preference.

I went to pay the fee to use the church a couple months before the wedding, and the church secretary, who knew my husband, asked me if I attended church. I told her no, but I had worked at both a Baptist church and a Jewish school while I was in college. I felt like that would soften the blow that I was not a church goer and was completely prepared for her to start judging me. I remember, though, that she very calmly and sweetly said, "It sounds like the Lord is trying to bring you back to Him."

I smiled politely, but in my head, I was thinking, "Or I was desperate for a job."

At the time, I had no idea how much my life would change in eight years. If this church secretary had told me that in eight years, I would be writing a Christian book, I don't think I could have smiled politely. I would have most likely laughed in her face. Yet that is how God works. If he can't reach you one way, He will reach you another way.

When I was talking to those who shared their testimonies, I couldn't help but think "My God, how amazing You are!" I knew what God had done in my life, but to hear testimony after testimony of God's love and grace was miraculous. There were many nights I cried tears of joy as I wrote. Some of these people were pulled out of the depths of their own personal hell while others were given a gentle nudge in the right direction. God reached each person in a way that was appropriate for their lives, and He worked miracles.

Each person who shared their testimony has had their own walk, their own timeline. There was no cookie cutter version. And guess what? Their stories are not finished. They will continue to face trials. They will continue to have triumphs. They may even get upset or frustrated with God, but they will also continue to feel God's love for them. They will continue to feel peace knowing that God gave his only son so that they could live forever with him in Heaven. They will feel His strength when they feel weak.

> "No evil befalls you, and a plague does not come near your tent; for He commands His messengers concerning you, to guard you in all your ways" (Ps. 91:10–11).

This comfort is not exclusive to them. You can have that comfort too. You can have God come into your life and change the very fabric of your being. You can feel a love so strong that everything else pales in comparison. You can feel strength in times you would normally crumble. You can have peace even during the most devastating moments of your life. You can forgive yourself for your sins and others who may have hurt you. You can feel whole for the first time in your life.

Are ready to be changed, to feel comfort, to forgive and be forgiven? If you feel that stirring in your soul, say this prayer.

Prayer of Salvation

Dear Heavenly Father, I ask You to come into my life to wash me clean of my sins. I ask for forgiveness of any past transgressions, and for You to guide me in the ways in which You want me to live my life. I ask for peace from my past. Allow me to forgive my misgivings, as You have forgiven me. Help me to repeatedly seek You first and to bring others the love You have shown me. Allow me to be a continual testament of your grace. You are my guiding light. Jesus died and lived again so that I may be saved. My former life is gone as I am made new through the blood of Your son, Jesus Christ, my Lord and Savior. I pray all of this in Jesus's mighty name. Amen!

Scripture References

1 Corinthians 10:13
1 Corinthians 15:33
1 John 1:9
1 John 4:7
1 John 5:15
1 Peter 4:8
1 Peter 5:6–7
1 Samuel 16:7
1 Timothy 1:14–16
2 Peter 3:9
2 Timothy 1:7
2 Timothy 3:14
Colossians 3:12
Colossians 3:13
Deuteronomy
6:5, 10–11
Ecclesiastes 3:1, 3, 7
Ephesians 2:10
Ephesians 4:15
Ephesians 4:26–28
Ephesians 4:31
Ephesians 4:32
Ephesians 5:8

Ephesians 5:13–16

Isaiah 43:18
Isaiah 44:22
James 1:2–4
James 4:10
Jeremiah 10:23
Jeremiah 29:11
Jeremiah 30:2
Jeremiah 31:3
Jeremiah 33:3
John 8:7
John 8:36
John 14:27
John 15:2
John 16:33

Joshua 1:9–11
Luke 4:5–6
Luke 6:37
Luke 15:10
Luke 15:32
Mark 1:17
Mark 11:25
Matthew 5:16

Matthew 7:1–2

Philippians 4:6–7
Proverbs 3:5–6
Proverbs 3:7
Proverbs 6:16–19
Proverbs 6:32
Proverbs 11:14
Proverbs 17:9
Proverbs 19:3
Proverbs 19:20
Proverbs 19:21
Proverbs 22:6
Proverbs 24:11
Proverbs 28:13
Proverbs 31:30

Psalms 34:18
Psalms 55:22
Psalms 56:12–13
Psalms 68:5
Psalms 90:17
Psalms 91:2
Psalms 91:10–11
Psalms 103:8–12
Psalms 115:1,
11–12, 14–15

Scripture References

Esther 4:14	Matthew 7:3	Psalms 147:5
Exodus 15:2	Matthew 7:7	Romans 3:23
Galatians 5:25	Matthew 7:13–14	Romans 5:3–4
Genesis 50:20	Matthew 11:28	Romans 5:8
Hebrews 4:12–13	Matthew 15:18	Romans 6:23
Hebrews 8:12	Matthew 18:12–13	Romans 8:2
Hebrews 12:11	Matthew 18:21–22	Romans 8:28
Isaiah 40:31	Philippians 3:12–14	Romans 12:2
	Philippians 4:13	Zephaniah 3:17

CPSIA information can be obtained
at www.ICGtesting.com
Printed in the USA
BVHW031310200221
600656BV00001B/8